D1519641

Aislinge Meic Conglinne

Medieval Studies

Mary Maleski, *Series Editor*

Aislinge Meic Conglinne

THE VISION OF MAC CONGLINNE

Translated and with an introduction by

Lahney Preston-Matto

SYRACUSE UNIVERSITY PRESS

First Edition 2010

10 11 12 13 14 15   6 5 4 3 2 1

For a listing of books published and distributed by Syracuse University Press,
visit our Web site at SyracuseUniversityPress.syr.edu.

ISBN: 978-0-5156-3218-4

Library of Congress Cataloging-in-Publication Data

Aislinge Meic Conglinne. English & Irish.

The vision of Mac Conglinne / translated and with an introduction
by Lahney Preston-Matto. — 1st ed.

p. cm.

Text in English and Irish.

Includes bibliographical references.

ISBN 978-0-8156-3218-4 (cloth : alk. paper)

1. Irish language—Middle Irish, 1100–1550—Texts.   2. Epic literature,
Irish—Translations into English.   3. Mythology, Celtic—Ireland.
4. Tales—Ireland.   I. Preston-Matto, Lahney.

PB1397.A37 2010

491.6'27—dc22   2010010134

CONTENTS

ACKNOWLEDGMENTS

My first debt of gratitude is to Greg Delanty, who provided the inspiration for the translation and the periodic reminders that I actually needed to finish! Mulligan's on Poolbeg Street saw the genesis of the idea for this translation, and Greg and I had great *craic* there and in other pubs in Dublin and New York discussing the text. I am grateful for his wisdom, expertise, and friendship.

Without Catherine McKenna's class in Old Irish and Pádraig Ó Cearúill's Modern Irish classes, I never would have been able to attempt this translation at all. Cathy Swift's summer course in Old and Middle Irish was of enormous use as a grounding in the history of the Irish language, and I am also indebted to the entire staff of the Dublin Institute for Advanced Studies 2008 Summer School.

My colleagues in the English Department at Adelphi University have been incredibly supportive; in particular, I would like to thank Kris Fresonke for her rigorous and constructive criticism of a very early draft, as well as editorial suggestions throughout. Judith Weiss and Sreedevi Satyavolu at the Swirbul Library cheerfully ordered pile upon pile of interlibrary loan material for me, and I am deeply grateful. A Faculty Development Award for 2008 enabled me to travel to Ireland, refresh my Old and Middle Irish, and work extensively on the manuscript.

ACKNOWLEDGMENTS

Karen Overbey and Maggie Williams offered incisive criticism and close readings of the introduction, and I have benefited immensely from their suggestions and their friendship.

Finally, I am thankful for my family, Michael, Brigid, and Arthur, and very much appreciate the time they've allowed me to spend away from them to write this book.

GUIDE TO PRONUNCIATION

Middle Irish may look intimidating, but its pronunciation is actually quite regular, far more regular, in fact, than English. First and foremost, the stress on any word falls on the first syllable.

Consonants are mostly as they appear in English, although they are usually softened when they appear in the middle or at the end of a word.

Consonant	At beginning of word sounds like:	In middle or at end of word sounds like:
B	B as in *boy*	V as in *heaven* or W as in *wood*
C, CC	C as in *cart*, never *circus*	G as in *frog*
CH	CH as in German *ich* or Scottish *loch*, never *church*	CH as in German *ich* or Scottish *loch*, never *church*
D	D as in *diver*	TH as in *though* (voiced)
G	G as in *gap*, never *germ*	GH as in German *Madgen*
M, MB, MM	M as in *mop*	V as in *heaven* or W as in *wood*
N, ND, NN	N as in *nod*	N as in *nod*
P	P as in *part*	B as in *scrub*

S, SS	S as in *sat*, never *raise* (before *a*, *o*, *u*, or after when final)	SH as in *sheet* (before *e* or *i*, or after when final)
T, TT	T as in *top*	D as in *odd*
TH	TH as in *thin*, never *though*	TH as in *thin*, never *though*

Vowels are similar to vowels in continental languages. When the vowel is in the unstressed portion of the word, it is almost always a schwa, called the obscure vowel, which sounds similar to *-uh:* small*e*r, past*a*, f*u*r, f*i*r, pist*o*l. In the stressed vowels, the following apply:

A, AI: f*a*ther
Á, ÁI: p*a*w
ÁE, AÍ: *ai*sle, but became simplified to str*ee*t
E, EI, ÉO, ÉOI: m*e*t
I: s*i*n
Í, ÍU, ÍUI: str*ee*t
ÍA, ÍAI: pleb*eia*n
O, OI: h*o*t
Ó, ÓI: n*o*te
ÓE, OÍ: s*oi*l, but became simplified to f*a*te
U, UI: p*u*t
Ú, ÚI: b*oo*t
Ú, ÚAI: p*oo*r

Introduction

Summary of the Tale

Aislinge Meic Conglinne, or "The Vision of Mac Conglinne," is an anonymous Middle Irish[1] romance, written in alternating prose and verse, and is therefore known as a prosimetric tale. The Middle Irish text contains a number of *hapax legomena* (sole instances of a word in a language) that already make the text significant. But *Aislinge Meic Conglinne* is also noteworthy for its depiction of the customs and values of medieval Ireland, particularly with reference to the church, political systems, and the arts, as well as more specific aspects of cultural status such as food, hospitality, and punishment for crimes. The narrative is typical of many medieval tales in its tendency to bypass exposition and character development. The text is linear and has a clear beginning, middle, and end, which

---

1. Irish, like English, has a number of temporal linguistic markers. The Old Irish period was ca. 600–900 CE; the Middle Irish period was ca. 900–1200 CE. Until relatively recently, little linguistic work has been done on Middle Irish. Kenneth Hurlstone Jackson was one of the pioneers in the field. See also Damian McManus's "History of the Language II: Middle Irish" (n.d.), Liam Breatnach's "An Mheán-Ghaeilge" (1994), and Kim McCone's chapter on Middle Irish in *The Early Irish Verb* (1997) and his section on Middle Irish in *A First Old Irish Grammar and Reader Including an Introduction to Middle Irish* (2005).

is more than can be said for many medieval texts, where manuscript condition often dictates what parts of the narrative remain. The only point at which the narrative could be seen as confusing is near the end, when Mac Conglinne recounts his vision to Cathal mac Finguine, king of Munster. Mac Conglinne actually relates two visions instead of one. These are different in genre—one is primarily verse, while the other is primarily prose—and subject matter, as the verse vision recounts Mac Conglinne's visit to a land of not earth, stones, and water but foodstuffs, and the prose version details Mac Conglinne's interactions with the Fáithliaig, the Witch Doctor who orders a specific course of treatment, involving the consumption of massive amounts of food. The text assumes intimate knowledge of the geography of Ireland, as well as an understanding of how specific cultural institutions such as kingship, the church, and the law function in medieval Ireland, for which this introduction provides some of the basic information required.

Even though the text is called "The Vision of Mac Conglinne," the main character of the tale is actually Cathal mac Finguine, king of Munster. Cathal mac Finguine was a historic king who ruled from 721 to 742 CE. He was one of the few Munster kings to oppose legitimately the hegemony of the Uí Néill dynasty in the North through tactical defense strategies and carefully selected forays into Uí Néill territory (see Byrne 2001, 205–11). In essence, Cathal attempted to limit the Uí Néill to its own territories in the northern half of the country, known as Leth Cuinn, or the Northern Half. In this text, however, Cathal has a "demon of gluttony" within him, which he swallowed when eating apples apparently sent to him by Lígach, the woman he wished to marry. However, Lígach had not sent the apples to Cathal at all: Lígach's brother Fergal cursed the apples and had them sent to Cathal as a gift from Lígach, because Fergal and Cathal were in contention for the kingship of Ireland. Fergal mac Máele

Dúin was the high-king of the North at this time; his sister Lígach would have been considered a fitting political match for Cathal mac Finguine as a way to cement cordial relations between Munster and Ulster. As a result of ingesting the "demon of gluttony," Cathal eats enormous amounts of food, literally devouring his kingdom.

Meanwhile, Anér Mac Conglinne, a monastic scholar, decides to give up his life of study in order to become a poet and to seek out Cathal mac Finguine, whom he has heard is generous to poets. On his way to Cathal, Mac Conglinne walks from Roscommon to Cork in a day—a highly improbable hike of approximately 120 miles—and stops at the guesthouse of Cork's monastery where he receives substandard hospitality. When he satirizes what he's been given in verse, the abbot of the monastery, Manchín, decides that the only appropriate punishment is to put Mac Conglinne to death. The monks strip and whip him, nearly drown him in the river, and lock him into the guesthouse overnight. In the morning, Mac Conglinne, through a variety of ruses and legal maneuverings, manages to delay his sentence until the evening, at which point he gains a respite overnight. During the night an angel appears and gives him a vision. He recounts his vision to the abbot the next morning, beginning with a genealogy of Manchín himself. This genealogy is not the standard one, however, but one that recounts Manchín's family in food; for example, "Son of Leek, so green-tailed / Son of Bacon, mac Butter" (see page 19, lines 380–81). The vision proper tells of a land made of food—a house of cheese and meat that must be rowed to on a lake of new milk in a boat made of lard, with a well of wine behind the house—and the abbot realizes that Mac Conglinne is the one who has been sent to cure Cathal mac Finguine of his demon. He releases Mac Conglinne on the condition that he will go to Cathal, and Mac Conglinne demands Manchín's cloak as payment for his services.

Mac Conglinne travels to Cathal, who is making a circuit of his subject kings who in turn are obliged to provide him with a certain number of feasts a year. When Mac Conglinne first meets Cathal, Cathal is in Pichán mac Moíle Finde's house eating bushels of apples. Pichán is the king of Iveagh, one of Cathal's subject kings. Mac Conglinne shames Cathal into sharing the apples with him and then requests a boon of Cathal, which is that he will fast with him overnight. The next day, Mac Conglinne will not let Cathal eat until preaching has been done. The fast lasts the entire day, and Mac Conglinne makes Cathal fast again for the second night. On the following day, Mac Conglinne orders Pichán to bring all the most savory meats that he has, and begins to cook them in front of a bound Cathal. While the food is cooking, Mac Conglinne recites two visions. The demon cannot withstand the double assault of the smell of the food cooking and Mac Conglinne's overwhelming verbal descriptions of alternative universes composed of food and leaps out of Cathal's mouth to carry off a piece of meat, at which point Mac Conglinne overturns a cooking vat on it. The demon of gluttony manages to escape, but Mac Conglinne reaps many spiritual and material rewards in addition to saving Cathal mac Finguine and his entire kingdom from what would certainly have become a famine.

SECULAR KINGS

Although the above summary illustrates that the text emphatically endorses the power of poetry and the poet, it is also necessary to understand that a poet's skills and talents were practiced in the service of a patron, generally a king. Cathal is the real protagonist of this tale, not Mac Conglinne; Cathal's needs and desires are catered to, with most of the other characters serving, in one way or another, to fulfill those needs and desires. Early Ireland was a hierarchical society, with clear distinctions between and among noble and common, free and not free, and kings were the highest-ranking members of early Irish society.[2] While there were many articulated ranks of kingship within early Ireland's social hierarchy, Cathal mac Finguine is depicted as *rí cóicid*, a provincial king.[3] Literally, the term means "king of a fifth," because there were five provinces of early medieval Ireland: Ulaid, now known as Ulster; Laigin, now known as Leinster; Connachta, now known as Connacht; Mumu, now known as Munster (of which province Cathal was king); and Mide, now known as Meath and no longer considered a province of its own. The *rí cóicid* was the highest level of kingship to be attained, with one exception: the sagas and annals mention very often a *rí Érenn*, or "king of Ireland," who would be highest of all in the hierarchy, but this title does not appear in the legal texts (F. Kelly 1988, 18). A provincial king, a *rí cóicid* such as Cathal, would have been the overlord of several lower-ranking kings: the *rí túath* or *ruiri*, which means "king of several *túaths*," and below that, the *rí túaithe*, the king of a *túath*, the smallest political unit at the time, generally understood as a petty kingdom. As a point of reference, from the fifth to the twelfth centuries there were approximately 150 kings in Ireland at any one time (Byrne 2001, 7).

2. This introduction can provide only a brief overview of the importance of the king to early Irish society, but the following are a good introduction to more in-depth analyses of Irish kingship: Bhreathnach 2005; Binchy 1970; Byrne 2001, 7–70; Dillon 1946; Jaski 2000; F. Kelly 1988, 17–26; McCone 1990, 107–37; and Wiley 2008.

3. Other names for the *rí cóicid* are the *ollam ríg* (greatest of kings) and the *rí ruirech* (king of overkings). See Byrne 2001, 41–42; and F. Kelly 1988, 17–18 for the variety of names employed for the different levels of kings.

Kings maintained their rank through personal wealth, measured in movable property and landownership. As wealthy men and extensive landowners, kings had all the typical responsibilities associated with Irish property ownership, such as maintaining clients on their land. There were also three quite specific aspects of kingship: they had to be beautiful, or at a minimum without physical defect; they needed wisdom and the perspicacity to render fair judgments; and they needed to be excellent warriors. Each of these aspects has a larger cultural significance: a perfect physical specimen is capable of fighting and producing an heir, the ability to rule fairly ensures a kingdom's stability, and prowess on the battlefield enhances the king's (and the kingdom's) reputation and increases the king's landholdings.

Most early Irish tales expend a great deal of energy stressing the beauty and perfection of the king hero of the tale. As one example, king of Ireland Conare Már in *Togail Bruidne Da Derga* (The Destruction of Da Derga's Hostel) is characterized as: "the most splendid and distinguished and handsome and powerful king who has ever come into the world. . . . There is no flaw in him, not as to form or shape or clothing, or size or arrangement or proportion, or eye or hair or whiteness, or wisdom or pleasingness or eloquence, or weapons or equipment or attire, or splendour or abundance or dignity, or bearing or prowess or ancestry" (Gantz 1981b, 91). Since the king is also expected to be a great warrior, a physical defect such as a missing limb would be an obvious deterrent to fulfilling part of his responsibilities. Famously, one of the kings of the Túatha dé Danann, Núadu Argetlám—Núadu of the Silver Hand—lost his limb in a battle, but had it restored with one of silver by a physician and was thus able to reclaim his throne. There are other blemishes that initially appear harmless that also negate a king's right to rule. For example, Congal Cáech (Congal the One-Eyed) was removed from the kingship of Tara when he was blinded by a bee sting. The later annals are full of references to kings blinding or otherwise mutilating their hostages—often the sons or nephews of their potential rivals—so that they are not eligible to take over as opposing king. The metaphoric significance of blinding is related to a king's ability to judge correctly—to be able to "see" all the aspects of a case before him and decide accordingly on the right course of action.

The first requirement of kingship discussed, physical perfection, thus overlaps with a second key feature of kingship, *fír flathemon,* the specific term used for the king's truth or judgment. And while *fír flathemon* does have to do with legal judgments, its scope is much broader. If a king was good, wise, and true, it was believed these traits had a ripple effect on the rest of the kingdom, so that everyone enjoyed peace and prosperity through great fertility of the land. A very early text from the eighth century, *Audacht Morainn* (The Testament of Morann), outlines what is expected of a king, some of which follows:

> It is through the justice of the ruler that plagues [and] great lightnings are kept from the people.
> It is through the justice of the ruler that he secures peace, tranquillity, joy, ease [and] comfort.
> It is through the justice of the ruler that he dispatches (great) battalions to the borders of hostile neighbours.
> It is through the justice of the ruler that abundances of great tree-fruit of the great wood are tasted.
> It is through the justice of the ruler that milk-yields of great cattle are maintained.
> It is through the justice of the ruler that there is abundance of every high, tall corn.
> It is through the justice of the ruler that abundance of fish swim in streams.

> It is through the justice of the ruler that fair children are well
> begotten. (F. Kelly 1976, 7)

The phrase that is repeated above, "it is through the justice of the
ruler," is written in Old Irish *is tre fhír flathemon,* and these state-
ments are clearly an illustration of how wide-ranging the effect of
a good ruler was believed to be in early Ireland. Similarly, in a tale
already discussed, "The Destruction of Da Derga's Hostel," the
beginning of King Conare's reign is eminently praiseworthy:

> There was great bounty, then, in Conare's reign: seven ships
> being brought to Indber Colptha in June of every year, acorns
> up to the knee every autumn, a surfeit over the Búas and the
> Bóand each June, and an abundance of peace, so that no one
> slew his neighbour anywhere in Ériu—rather, that neighbour's
> voice seemed as sweet as the strings of harps. From the middle of
> spring to the middle of autumn, no gust of wind stirred any cow's
> tail; there was no thunder, no stormy weather in Conare's reign.
> (Gantz 1981b, 67)

Again, what is stressed about a true king is that he brings peace and
fertility to the lands he rules, thereby ensuring the continuation of
his people.

Fír flathemon, while it refers to the king's truth or justice,
does not necessarily refer to justice in the strictly legal sense with
which we tend to associate it. A king was not solely responsible for
making legal decisions; he always had a judge and occasionally a
highly placed cleric to advise him. Indeed, a king may have simply
announced a judgment that was formulated by a judge or judges.
But the king was responsible, of course, for observing and enforc-
ing the laws (see F. Kelly 1988, 22–26). And if the king failed in

any of his responsibilities, particularly in his *fír flathemon,* he could be removed from his kingship. A breach of *fír flathemon* was called *gáu flathemon,* which means "falsehood of ruler/sovereignty." An apt example of both *fír flathemon* and *gáu flathemon* is provided in the story *Cath Maige Mucrama* (The Battle of Mag Mucrama). In this tale, Lugaid mac Con is the king of Tara and has taken as a foster son Cormac mac Airt, a prominent figure in the saga material. Lugaid is asked to make a judgment about some sheep that have eaten the queen's *glassen,* or woad plants:

> "I pronounce," said Mac Con, "that the sheep [be forfeited] for it." Cormac, a little boy, was on the couch beside him. "No, foster-father," said he, "the shearing of the sheep for the crop-ping of the *glassen* would be more just, for the *glassen* will grow [and] the wool will grow on the sheep."
>
> "That is the true judgement," said all. "Moreover, it is the son of the true prince [*mac na fírfhlatha*] who has given it."
>
> With that one side of the house falls down the cliff, namely the side in which the false judgement was given. . . .
>
> After that he [Lugaid mac Con] was a year in the kingship of Tara and no grass came through the earth, nor leaf on tree, nor grain in corn. So the men of Ireland expelled him from his king-ship for he was an unlawful ruler [*anfhlaith*]. (O Daly 1975, 59)

Bad judgments affect not only the king himself, in the loss of his kingdom (and part of his house!) but also his people, who here suf-fered through a year of famine. In contrast, Cormac is shown mak-ing a proper judgment even at a very young age; he will then be given the kingship of Tara after Lugaid's departure.

The final requirement of a king is that he exhibit military prow-ess. Any king must be able to maintain his borders and, if he has right on his side, increase the size of his holdings. Irish kings go into battle alongside fighters; they do not recuse themselves from the fighting and watch from a safe distance, planning strategy. In the many different annals kept in Ireland, there is hardly a year that goes by that does not mention the death of a king in battle. In the early literature, too, kings are always depicted as going to war. Cú Chulainn, hero of the *Táin Bó Cúailnge,* must find his king, Conchobar, on the battlefield and resuscitate him with an entire roast pig. Conare, king of Tara in *Togail Bruidne Da Derga* (The Destruction of Da Derga's Hostel), is the consummate warrior, as explained by Fer Rogain, who is detailing Conare's attributes to Conare's adversary, Ingcél:

> Six hundred will fall by him before he reaches his weapons, and once he has obtained his weapons, six hundred more will fall at the first onslaught. . . . There are nine entrances to the house, and at each entrance one hundred heroes will fall, and when everyone has stopped fighting, it is then that he will be performing feats of arms. If he encounters you outside the hostel, as numerous as hailstones or blades of grass or stars in the sky will be your cloven heads and cloven skulls and heaps of entrails that he crushes after he has scattered you about the ridges. (Gantz 1981b, 91–92)

Although being a good warrior was undoubtedly important, *Audacht Morainn* acknowledges that warfare is not something to be considered lightly. Part of the advice offered to the prince is: "Tell him, let him not redden many fore-courts, for bloodshed is a vain destruction of all rule and of protection from the kin for the ruler. Tell him, let him give any reciprocal service which is due from him, let him enforce any bond which he should bind, let him remove the shame of his cheeks by arms in battle against other territories, against their oath, against all their protections" (F. Kelly 1976, 11). A ruler should not go to war indiscriminately but should do so only in order to fulfill a bond or promise of service (to an overking, perhaps) or to avenge being shamed.

Because of early Ireland's stringent hierarchical structure, there were very clear expectations of a king, as his people depended upon him. Reciprocally, the king had expectations of his people. The lowest grade of king, the *rí túaithe,* was also a lord who had clients, and many of those clients would have clients of their own, depending on their rank. The basic relationship of lord to client involved the lord advancing land or livestock to his client in return for food-rent, winter hospitality, manual labor in the form of annual reaping and construction of fortifications for the lord's house, and military service for various events: hunting thieves or wolves, patrolling borders and strategic points, or going to war against another *túath.* In return, the client received, in addition to the material he was advanced, legal support from his lord. The amount of material advanced to the client depended on his status—a higher-status client received more material—and the amount that the client owed annually to the lord was proportional to how much he was given (F. Kelly 1988, 29–33). Particularly relevant for our tale is the winter hospitality due to a lord. When Mac Conglinne set out from Cork to find Cathal mac Finguine, Cathal was on his way to visit one of his underkings, Pichán mac Moíle Finde, in order to receive his winter feast, which was due to the lord between New Year's Day and Shrovetide, the several days preceding Lent; the lord could bring a large party with him (ibid., 30). Pichán was understandably upset about this particular winter feast, as the amount of food he believed Cathal would consume surpassed whatever profit Pichán might have made on his advance.

To some extent, the entire text of *Aislinge Meic Conglinne* is a commentary on hospitality: proper hospitality is infrequently proffered, and that irregularity threatens social disorder. For example, a lack of generosity was considered a sign of a bad king, one way a king could ruin his people and culture. Travelers relied on the hospitality of strangers, regardless of status, but particularly on high-ranking members of society such as nobility and clerics. But in *Aislinge Meic Conglinne*, Mac Conglinne as a solitary traveler receives a shoddy welcome from the monastery at Cork, and a similarly poor one from Cathal mac Finguine. Generosity is part of the cultural bedrock of early Ireland, and in our text characters either refuse to proffer hospitality or resent their obligation to do so, in the case of Pichán's feast for Cathal. These refusals and resentments threaten social stability to such an extent that Mac Conglinne must negotiate an appropriate payment for Cathal's exorcism with three separate parties—the Cork monastery, Pichán, and Cathal himself—instead of confidently awaiting a shower of gifts.

Although Manchín and Cathal were undoubtedly wrong to refuse Mac Conglinne acceptable entertainment, they may have thought he was trying to take advantage of the hospitality system; anyone perceived to be doing so was particularly reviled. By and large, such abuses of the system would have been perpetrated by travelers across provincial or *túath* borders, although traveling in itself was slightly unusual in that most people in early Ireland did not have legal rights beyond their own *túath:* only poets, clergy, lawyers, and kings—in other words, the learned classes—were allowed to travel freely (F. Kelly 1988, 5). Clergy, in particular, could travel and be assured of finding a place to stay with their brethren. Poets such as Mac Conglinne, however, could not travel with the same amount of certainty. In addition, Mac Conglinne's status is ambiguous: at the beginning of the text he is a clerical student and gives up his studies to pursue poetry, but he is not yet any recognized grade of poet during his travels. Early Irish saga material is littered with references to wicked poets who are nothing more than freeloaders, with hosts desperate to be rid of them. In *Cath Maige Tuired* (The Second Battle of Mag Tuired), a famous warrior named the Dagda is daily importuned by a blind, idle satirist poet named Cridenbél for the three best bits of his meal. The Dagda is advised to put one piece of gold into each of the three best bits of his meal, and Cridenbél dies from ingesting them. The Dagda is able to defend himself by illustrating that Cridenbél's overwhelming greed caused his death (Gray 1982, 29, 31). Similarly, the church was often the victim of guests who made themselves at home for too long. The Irish life of Coemgen relates that musicians asked for food from Coemgen when he had none. He asked them to wait, but they would not and began insulting him. In retaliation, their wooden instruments were turned to stone (Plummer 1968b, 1:129, 2:125). Poets and other practitioners of occupations that relied on travel, then, were generally stereotyped as abusers of hospitality.

And while abuses of generosity certainly took place, it was still a cultural expectation; the monastery, Pichán, and Cathal mac Finguine are criticized throughout the text for their lack of it. Both Pichán and Cathal are kings, which further underscores how important it was for kings to be generous. Pichán is terrified of the quantities of food that Cathal consumes, and for his part, Cathal refuses to share food with anyone, including persons close to him in his retinue. The monks in Cork's monastery do not provide enough food or a comfortable-enough place to stay to keep body and soul together. Even though poets may have been seen as abusive and insufficiently appreciative guests by the Cork monastery, it was not right to judge Mac Conglinne as abusive sight unseen, nor was it appropriate to deny him standard care, to say nothing of whipping and threatening

to crucify him. Pichán is also judgmental: when offered Mac Cong-
linne's assistance in curing Cathal, he seriously underestimates how
much that assistance is worth. And Cathal does not seem to com-
prehend the effect that his stinginess and perceived greediness will
have on his reputation as king. Mac Conglinne must shame him into
sharing, into fulfilling his responsibility to be openhanded.

Aislinge Meic Conglinne, then, shows us the negative image of
hospitality: the reader is repeatedly told what is missing in the way
of hospitality, when it should be offered freely. In Mac Conglinne's
visions, generosity is illustrated when people in positions of high
authority, such as the Fáithliaig, the Witch Doctor, prescribe food
as the cure for all ills. These demonstrations set an example for real
life, that kings and other wealthy individuals such as the abbots
of monasteries should also offer food freely. Doing so will ensure
reciprocal services on the part of those individuals lower down in
the social hierarchy. Mac Conglinne is not only a satirist but also a
social conservative, calling for the restoration of true hospitality and
its attendants, fealty and kingship.

RELIGION AND POLITICS

By far the greatest corrupter of the expectations for hospitality and
generosity in our text is the Cork monastery. Manchín the abbot
is portrayed as unnecessarily vindictive, violent, and arrogant, and
these characteristics progress from bad to worse when his monks
desire alternatives to his demands, gently challenging his authority.
In many ways, the relationship between an abbot and his monks was
similar to the relationship between a king and his clients. Abbots
and kings demanded absolute authority and loyalty in return for
confident leadership that led to increased prosperity and human
resources. Since both kings and abbots saw themselves as the rulers

of their own territories, and those territories of necessity overlapped, questions about jurisdiction understandably arose. Did a king as secular political leader have authority over the church establishments on his land? Or did an abbot as spiritual leader wield more influence over the secular political sphere? Was there a functioning interrelationship between kings and monasteries? In our text, although Manchín directs Mac Conglinne to Cathal mac Finguine, there is no further indication of an extensive relationship between the two separate leaders. Nevertheless, the church, and Cork's monastery in particular, plays a vital role in the tale.

The church was firmly established in Ireland in the eighth century. In her groundbreaking survey of the church in early Ireland, Kathleen Hughes (1966) argues that the strict monasticism of the early Irish church became increasingly secularized, and was therefore fundamentally different from other Christian institutions that had an episcopal government. According to Hughes, the establishment of bishops and archbishops did not occur in Ireland until the Synod of Ráith Bressail in 1111, although there were earlier bishops appointed for Dublin and other Hiberno-Norse establishments by the archbishop of Canterbury. More recent studies by scholars such as Etchingham (1999), Mac Shamhráin (1996), and Sharpe (1992) have argued, however, that the Irish church was well acquainted with and accustomed to episcopal forms of organization for a much longer period of time than previously recognized. Additionally, all three have argued that there was a much deeper secular dynastic influence on the organization of the church than previously thought. The relationship between kings as secular political rulers and abbots of monasteries as religious rulers was deeply interconnected in the eighth century, when the action in our text is meant to take place.

There are many examples of cooperation between individual monasteries and the local political dynasties in the eighth century, but both the church and the local king necessarily believed that their claim on the people of the *túath* should be strongest. They struggled over physical and spiritual claims to the people, but also limited resources. Monasteries could be as wealthy as the local king, making themselves attractive to local dynasties; they were the closest thing to an urban space that existed, and so attracted tradespeople and farmers with their families. Monasteries produced valuable items such as manuscripts, and the tradespeople in their workshops produced ecclesiastical artwork—chalices, reliquaries, stone crosses, croziers—and the churches that housed the artwork. In the current understanding of the relationship between political dynasties and individual monasteries, particular focus has been placed on the abbatial office; the abbot of a monastery and the local political ruler were often closely related.[4] As Ailbhe Mac Shamhráin notes: "The reality of dynastic intervention at many of the larger ecclesiastical settlements has long been understood, even if its full extent may yet have to be realised. It is widely accepted that ruling lineages commonly sought to exploit the economic resources of ecclesiastical settlements, in some instances using them as political powerbases. One outcome of this was the marked politicisation of the abbatial office that has been observed at several major ecclesiastical centres" (1996, 216). In an attempt to solidify their political power local dynastic rulers sought to place their close blood relations (brothers, sons, nephews, and so on) as abbots within the local monasteries. Alternatively, if faced with a lack of male relatives willing to join the church, the kings tried to intervene in the monasteries' business for their own profit.

4. See, for example, Mac Shamhráin 1996; Ó Corráin 1973; Etchingham 1999; Sharpe 1992; Herbert 1996; McCone 1990; and Bitel 1990.

Introduction

The Uí Néill are the best-known example of cooperation between secular political dynasties and the church. The Uí Néill were located in Ulster (Ulaid in medieval Ireland) and Meath (Mide in medieval Ireland) and were divided into two branches, the Northern Uí Néill and the Southern Uí Néill. Each of these branches was further subdivided, the Northern Uí Néill represented by the Cenél nEógain and the Southern Uí Néill by Clann Cholmáin; these two subdivisions alternated the high-kingship of Ireland between them. Clann Cholmáin were also the hereditary holders of the sacral kingship of Tara, in Meath, and the position of high-king developed with kingship of Tara as a prerequisite. High-kings were most active from the ninth to the eleventh centuries, for all intents and purposes coming to an end with Brian Bóruma's defeat at Clontarf in 1014, although there were several high-kings "with opposition" in the eleventh and twelfth centuries. And although a high-king does not exist in the legal codes, these laws were mostly codified in the eighth century. The high-king is described extensively in the literary and annalistic material, but the concept of a high-king was introduced, in all likelihood, from the monasteries of Iona and Armagh and their interactions with the secular kings of Britain (Byrne 2001, 257–60). Armagh, located in Northern Uí Néill territory, created primacy for itself above all other monasteries in Ireland by asserting its status as the base of Saint Patrick, credited with establishing Christianity in Ireland, and his heirs. The Uí Néill provided not only high-kings for Ireland but also bishops for Armagh, and Armagh's scriptorium produced many works of propaganda linking the Uí Néill with Saint Patrick. Armagh emphasized the Uí Néill's importance politically, and its own importance religiously, thus granting this region of Ireland, Ulster and Meath, precedence over every other part of the island. It is not surprising, then, that Armagh should be mentioned in our tale, although physically removed from the action of the tale.

Just because Armagh and the Uí Néill worked very hard to present themselves as preeminent does not mean that no one challenged them. Cathal mac Finguine challenged the Uí Néill king Fergal mac Máele Dúin in 721, with the help of the Leinster king Murchad mac Brain. Fergal went on in the following year to attack Leinster—which led to his death—but Cathal did not support Murchad at this time, suggesting that Cathal was not interested in uniting the southern half of Ireland under his leadership. The *Annals of Inisfallen* note that Fergal submitted to Cathal in 721, but this report was probably not accurate; more likely, Fergal and Cathal made peace. In the 730s Cathal again made incursions into Uí Néill territory, but nothing serious came of it. And although he tried to take advantage of Leinster, the province had suffered such a crushing defeat at the hands of the Uí Néill that Cathal could not make headway to unite southern Ireland under his direction. While Cathal was certainly invested in challenging the secular political authority of the Uí Néill, he did not extend to the church his questioning of authority. In 737 Cathal met with Áed Allán, the king of the Uí Néill, after which it is noted that the law of Patrick was enforced throughout Ireland. This entry could be interpreted as Cathal's recognizing Armagh's supremacy among the churches in Ireland, but it also clearly demonstrates the attempt to construct a universal religious law throughout all Ireland, made possible only with the necessary support of the king of Munster and the other provincial kings (Byrne 2001, 207–9).

Byrne notes that there were only three Munster kings who offered serious opposition to the political hegemony of the Uí Néill and attendant religious supremacy of Armagh: Cathal mac Finguine, who ruled from 723 to 742; Feidlimid mac Crimthainn from 820 to 841; and Cormac mac Cuilennáin in the early tenth century (2001, 203). Cathal has been discussed above, but the two later kings represented a more integrated approach to the claims of secular and religious politics: Feidlimid mac Crimthainn and Cormac mac Cuilennáin were both ecclesiastics and kings (as was Flaithbertach mac Inmainén, who succeeded Cormac in 908) (ibid., 214). There were also *rí túaithe* who served as abbots of monasteries in Munster. The writer of *Aislinge Meic Conglinne* would have been well aware of this tradition of ecclesiastical kings in Munster history. As one example, Feidlimid mac Crimthainn was a founder of the Céli Dé movement, one that sought to bring an ascetic reform to the ninth-century church. Sources disagree as to whether he was a priest, but regardless, he was important as both a religious and a secular political ruler. As king of Munster, during his rule he continually opposed the Uí Néill; additionally, Feidlimid was known for attacking monasteries and burning entire foundations. Violence was an obviously accepted method for negotiating secular political power, and was used equally by seekers of religious political authority. Kathleen Hughes argues that Feidlimid "was responsible during his reign (820–847) for more violence towards the church than any other Irishman" (1966, 192). He burned and looted at least four monasteries, imprisoned the abbot of Cork and let him die without communion, and took over the abbacies of Clonfert and Cork. But he reserved particular animosity for Clonmacnois, where he murdered the entire *familia* and burned the establishment twice. Byrne argues that he destroyed only those monasteries that were a potential threat to Armagh's supremacy—hence his focus on Clonmacnois, one of Armagh's chief rivals—as he set his sights on the high-kingship of Ireland, administered from Cashel, with Armagh's support (2001, 220). There was also traditional hostility between Munster and Clonmacnois on account of the monastery's refusal to appoint a Munster abbot after the early seventh century (ibid., 171).

THE PLACES OF *AISLINGE MEIC CONGLINNE*

As is clear from such examples of violence stemming from geographical allegiances, and as in many medieval Irish texts, geography is particularly important in *Aislinge Meic Conglinne.* Geographical sites and onomastics are of course related to political, religious, and economic power, and *Aislinge Meic Conglinne* makes a strong argument for Cork and its environs as a spiritual and political center in Ireland. This text, then, may be trying to solidify Munster's, and Cork's, reputation. Today, Ireland is divided into four sections or provinces: Munster in the South, Leinster in the East, Connacht in the West, and Ulster in the North. Early Ireland was divided into fifths: the four provinces above, with the addition of Meath, located between Ulster and Leinster, and headed by the kingship of Tara. Most of the action in our tale takes place in Cork, which is in Munster, and at Pichán mac Moíle Finde's kingdom, also in Munster. Because the kings of the Uí Néill dynasties were able to consolidate power and gain the control over the high-kingship of Ireland, their main provinces, Ulster and Meath, tend to be discussed most frequently in the early literature. *Aislinge Meic Conglinne* seeks to remove some of that hegemony and increase Munster's reputation in the literary canon.

Increasing Munster's reputation would also serve to improve Leth Moga's reputation. Medieval Ireland was conceptualized as split in half; Ulster, Connacht, and Meath were the northern half, and Munster and Leinster were the southern half, with "a line between Dublin and Galway Bay" serving as the dividing point (ibid., 168). The northern half was called Leth Cuinn and the southern Leth Moga, or Conn's Half and Mug's/Mog's Half. This boundary was political, not ecclesiastical, although the Uí Néill, who were the rulers of Leth Cuinn, were continually trying to expand into Leth Moga, and also to extend Armagh's influence throughout both halves.

Our text emphasizes Leth Moga throughout and concentrates on Cork geography in particular. In this focus it is not unusual, as there were other texts written during the same time frame that also emphasized Cork, such as the hagiography of Saint Finbarr, Cork's patron saint. Saint Finbarr, also known as Barra, established all his churches and performed all his works in the environs of Cork in the seventh century, making Cork famous.[5] His followers were instrumental in uniting his scattered churches to form a coherent unit in the face of Viking attacks in the early ninth century (ibid., 224). Repeatedly in the vernacular life of Barra we are told that various monasteries and nunneries throughout Munster "placed their churches under perpetual obligation to God and to Barra," thus offering Barra their loyalty and obedience (Ó Riain 1994, 69). Barra's life was not written until the end of the twelfth century in all probability, although he lived in the late sixth and early seventh centuries (ibid., 33). In *Aislinge Meic Conglinne,* which was probably written before Barra's hagiography, Saint Finbarr is recognized by Manchín, the abbot of Cork's monastery, as his patron saint. Our text may exhibit a continued effort to promote Barra's importance in Cork, just as his monasteries united their efforts under his name in the ninth century.

Although the reminders of Saint Finbarr in *Aislinge Meic Conglinne* may help to underline the importance of Cork and its status as head of the ecclesiastical hierarchy in Munster, the text may also be seen as an attempt to mock Munster's political aspirations

5. This point is primarily true of Barra's vernacular life; his Latin life, on the contrary, seeks to avoid too much geographical specificity. See Ó Riain 1994, 92.

to greatness by portraying it as ruled by a sinful king, possessed by a demon. Additionally, Cork's desire to be seen as the preeminent religious establishment in Munster is questioned, as the monastery is assigned an overly vindictive spiritual leader who took umbrage at the slightest provocation. The king of Munster at the time *Aislinge Meic Conglinne* was written, from the late eleventh to the early twelfth centuries, was Muirchertach Ua Briain. Muirchertach was also high-king of Ireland "with opposition" and is remembered for his generous donation of Cashel to the church in Ireland in 1101 at the Synod of Cashel. Previously, Cashel had been both a religious and a political stronghold, but with Muirchertach's gift, it became a wholly religious base. This fact was emphasized in 1111 at the Synod of Ráith Bressail, at which a regularized diocesan system was first instituted in Ireland, and Cashel was named as the second metropolitan see behind Armagh (Byrne 2001, 191–92; Hughes 1966, 263). Muirchertach, like the historical Cathal mac Finguine, had the ambition to take over the high-kingship of Ireland as a Munsterman instead of as an Uí Néill; further, he had the temerity to try to influence the church's decisions about which of its establishments was most important. Muirchertach was also no stranger to propaganda; he was the patron of *Cogadh Gaedhel re Gallaibh,* or *The War of the Gaedhil with the Gaill,* which describes Munster's glorious Brian Bóruma (Muirchertach's great-grandfather) and his ascension to the high-kingship of Ireland and war with the Vikings. Our text, then, may have been written by someone interested in checking Munster's and its rulers' ambitions, particularly considering that although Mac Conglinne himself is described as a Munsterman, he is also affiliated with Ulster. In the introductory poem explaining his name he hails from Ulster, and he leaves from Armagh to go to Cork. In another manuscript of the tale, known as the H text (see below for further information about the manuscript history of the text), he is an Ulsterman throughout, studying at Armagh. The writer may be illustrating Ulster's supremacy—including the Uí Néill and Armagh—over Munster and its aspirations to "national" prominence in his choice of a main protagonist of comparably low status who is able to best a provincial king and the abbot of one of Munster's leading monasteries.

The Poets' Role in Medieval Ireland

Mac Conglinne's role as an intermediary between the ecclesiastical hierarchy and the local political hierarchy is downplayed within the text but is important. Relations between the Christian church and local kings were by turns tranquil and cooperative, as discussed above, and could be fraught with conflict and competition over property and followers. As abbot of the monastery of Cork, Manchín is the most powerful local member of the church. Manchín's ecclesiastical power is balanced against the authority of the provincial Munster king, Cathal mac Finguine. At the beginning of the tale Mac Conglinne is a religious scholar, a *scolaige,* and thus affiliated with a monastery and the life of the church, but he gives up this vocation to pursue the profession of poet. In terms of social status, this transition could be seen as a lateral move. As a scholar, Mac Conglinne had a certain amount of cachét that he gave up to become a student of poetry. *Uraicecht na Ríar,* an early (eighth-century) text on the poetic grades in early Irish law, makes clear that the status of a high-ranking poet is equivalent to the rank of a king, but the lower grades of poets have a much lower social standing. In early Ireland there were two different kinds of poets: the *filid,* who had an established career path that they could ascend by increasing their knowledge and their number of poetic compositions, and the *baird,* who were dependent for their status not on their poetic ability but on their previously established ranks in society. There were seven grades for each kind of poet, and with the *baird*, for example, there were categories such as *tigernbard*, a poet and a lord, and *rígbard*, a king and a poet. As Liam Breatnach, the editor of *Uraicecht na Ríar*, points out, "Nowhere . . . do we find mention of the bards progressing from grade to grade" (1987, 88). The *filid* do move up the ladder from grade to grade, though. The highest-ranking grade of the *filid*, the *ollam*, has "three hundred and fifty compositions, that is fifty for each grade; he is knowledgeable in all historical science, and he is knowledgeable in the jurisprudence of the law. His honour-price is forty *sét*s" (ibid., 103). Forty *sét*s is the equivalent of fourteen *cumal*s, which is what a *rí cóicid*, or provincial king, is worth. A *rí túaithe* is worth seven *cumal*s, according to *Críth Gablach*, which is approximately what the *anrúth*, the second-highest grade of *filid*, is worth (F. Kelly 1988, 17; Breatnach 1987, 109). The lowest grade of *filid*, the *fochloc*, had an honor price of one and a half *sét*s, but would have to have thirty compositions (Breatnach 1987, 111). There is no indication in our text that Mac Conglinne has been accepted into the ranks of *filid;* nowhere is he called by any of the titles accorded to the grades of the *filid*. Neither does he seem to have joined the ranks of the *baird*, as he is never accorded any of their titles, either. So he is just a student here as well, although he does seem to have a knack for composing satires and verses on the spot. Because he is not highly placed in the social hierarchy, it is surprising that he is allowed access to Cathal mac Finguine so easily, but perhaps desperate times call for desperate measures.

If Mac Conglinne were of a higher poetic grade, he could be a reasonable intermediate between Cathal mac Finguine and Manchín. As it is, he is sent from Manchín to Cathal, much as a servant would be sent on an errand. His status is somewhat questionable, even if his knowledge is not. The reader can tell that Mac Conglinne has access to knowledge of things above his social status, because he is able to compose satires and poems, and because he calls upon the legal institutions of guarantees, sureties, and bonds to ensure that Manchín, Pichán mac Moíle Finde, and Cathal mac Finguine all fulfill their vows to him. Both judges and poets were of *nemed,* or privileged, status, and were certainly relied upon by kings, if not so often by clerics. Ultimately, it seems, Mac Conglinne aspires to a status above what he possesses in the text and is successful in the end because the rewards he is given increase his wealth and therefore move him up the social hierarchy.

SATIRE IN MEDIEVAL IRELAND

Kings and abbots could use various tools to elicit beneficial results in any dispute: kings could impose economic sanctions or display military might, and abbots could also impose economic sanctions and the spiritual threat of excommunication and damnation. Poets, though, had one main weapon at their disposal: satire, which could "legally be used by a *fili* [poet] to exert pressure on a wrongdoer to get him to obey the law" (F. Kelly 1988, 49). Satire could be used only under certain circumstances, however; it was considered such a dangerous tool that its use was highly regulated. Satire's general intent is didactic and corrective; by pointing out the flaws in a person, institution, or belief system, satire calls attention to and demands their amendment. Throughout our text, Mac Conglinne alternates between satirizing those individuals who do him wrong, such as the monks of Cork, and praising those persons whose honor he wishes to increase, such as Cathal. In the case of Cathal, in fact, Mac Conglinne must both embarrass and praise him in order to achieve his goal of ridding Cathal of the demon of gluttony. He must also convince Cathal to fast with him in order to entice the demon of gluttony out of hiding.

Although satire in early Ireland had a distinctly legal purpose, it
also had a broader semantic application in the culture. For example,
one of the words for satire, *áer*, meant both "cutting, incising,"
and "act of satirizing, lampooning, defaming" (*Dictionary of the
Irish Language* 1983). In early Irish literature, satire was used to
inflict physical injury upon its recipient, often in the form of a blush,
or, more rarely, actual cuts on the cheeks, and, occasionally, death.
If the victim of satire was a king, this kind of injury could mean
the end of his rule, as physically imperfect kings were not allowed
to keep their kingdoms. So, for example, in the tale of Néide and
Caíar as edited by Whitley Stokes in *Three Irish Glossaries*, Néide
raises three blisters, "Stain, Blemish and Defect" on Caíar's cheeks
by reciting a satire against him (2000, xxxvi–xl).[6] Caíar was king
of Connacht, and Néide was his nephew and adopted son; Caíar's
wife desired Néide and promised him Caíar's reign if he would sleep
with her. As a result of Néide's satire, Caíar lost the kingship and
Néide became king. But Néide was fittingly punished for making
the wrongful satire: feeling remorseful, Néide pursued Caíar, who
ran away from him. When Caíar did see Néide, he "died for shame,"
and the rock under which he had been hiding fragmented, a piece
of which "pierced into [Néide's] head" (ibid., xxxix). The utter dev-
astation that satire could wreak is also reflected in "The Wooing
of Luaine," an early tale about King Conchobor of Ulster. Luaine,
betrothed to Conchobor, was asked to betray the king by Aithirne
and his two sons, famous satirists. (Aithirne is such a figure of terror
that he is described in "The Siege of Howth" as "a man who asked
the one-eyed for his single eye, and who used to demand the woman

6. See also Liam Breatnach's translation of the quatrain of satire in *Uraicecht
na Ríar* (1987, 115).

in child-bed" [Stokes 1887, 49].) She refused, and they satirized her, leaving three blotches on her cheeks, "namely Stain and Blemish and Disgrace, which were black and red and white. And thereupon the maiden died of shame" (Stokes 1903, 279). As with Néide, though, Aithirne's use of satire in this instance was improper, and Conchobor burned him and his family in their home.

Because satire in early Ireland was greatly feared as a possibly fatal weapon, it was therefore highly regulated. According to the *Corpus Iuris Hibernici,* the compilation of Irish law texts, "there are seven kinds of satire in Irish law for which compensation is estimated: a nickname which sticks; a recited satire; defaming in one's absence; satirizing to the face; laughter on both sides; appearance-mockery; making known a blemish" (Binchy 1978, 1:29.17–31.5; translation McLaughlin 2008, 52–53). As Vivian Mercier notes, it is often difficult for today's reader to tell the difference between many of these categorizations, but a lack of hospitality is frequently the cause for the creation of a satire (1962, 108–20, 118). For instance, the example that is given for a nickname that sticks is of a church in Mag nUlad. "Les Mór was its name at first, until the household of Les Mór Mo-Chutu came then to that church and a miserable, small meal was given to them. They ate quickly then and went to another place, and a nickname was bestowed upon that church, i.e. Church of the Wretched Meal" (McLaughlin 2008, 52–53). Certainly, a lack of hospitality is what causes Mac Conglinne to satirize the monastery in Cork and to embarrass Cathal at Pichán mac Moíle Finde's.

Food as Vehicle for Satire in the Tale

Food served to guests was an integral part of hospitality. Part of being a good host meant understanding what guests could and could not eat. For example, ecclesiastical canons had much to say about religious practice, hospitality, and food: "The ninth-century *Canones Adomnani* (Canons of Adomnán) . . . prohibits the consumption of meat that came from an animal that has drowned or plummeted to its death. . . . Eating cattle that had been seized in a raid was also forbidden. Powerful kings and chieftains would have had to find a way to surmount this prohibition, as it was common practice for them to serve at their feasts the meat that came from enemy spoils" (O'Sullivan 2004, 20).

Canones Adomnani are also quite specific about what constituted carrion: "Marine animals cast upon the shores, the nature of whose death we do not know, are to be taken for food in good faith, unless they are decomposed," but "animals that have died in water are carrion, since their blood remains within them" (Bieler 1963, 177). The attention paid to food in the laws is illustrative of its importance in the social hierarchy. Just as there was a clear and definable difference in the social status of a king and one of his clients, there was a corresponding difference in status among different types of food. When kings went to their clients for their winter feasts, they expected to be fed in large quantities with high-quality food. Average people seeking hospitality at a monastery could not anticipate the quality or quantity of food that a king might receive, but knew that they were entitled to it nonetheless, depending on their status.

In our text, food is the foundational architecture of the society: in Mac Conglinne's visions, footpaths are made of butter and palisades of pork. Food even replaces natural phenomena because the rivers flow with beer and the sand pours honey. Food is foundational also in that it reflects cultural health: we know that there is something terribly wrong with Cathal mac Finguine and his entire kingdom because he cannot treat food normally. And food identifies social status. All the food mentioned in the text was highly processed: as William Sayers notes, "few of the foodstuffs are in their natural raw state and all have passed through some form of cultural treatment, if only the separation of milk" (1994, 8). Bacon takes curing, wine and beer require fermenting, butter needs churning. Food that has been subjected to fire—including roasted meat, bread (particularly bread made of white flour), and custards and porridges—has always been an indicator of a civilized society; the more work a certain type of food takes to prepare, the more civilized that culture is. So the food mentioned as constituting boats and houses in our tale points to a labor-intensive, costly, civilized culture. Instead of using natural resources such as timber, iron, and stone, food is refined to build the structures of society, with the added benefit of being edible as well as attractive and supportive. Conversely, raw and unrefined foods indicate barbarity. As Claude Lévi-Strauss points out, the difference between the raw and the cooked is fundamental to human life and is seen as mirroring the difference between nature and culture (1969, 330–42).

Additionally, every society has what it considers high-status and low-status foods. In his recent book *Collapse: How Societies Choose to Fail or Succeed,* Jared Diamond discusses medieval Greenland and its colonization by the Norse, first begun in the late tenth and early eleventh centuries. The Irish were no strangers to the Norse, who had begun their Viking invasions of Ireland in the ninth century and established settlements, one of them Dublin, by the tenth century. Diamond argues that the Norse who settled Greenland did not eat fish because it was seen as a lower-status food. This fact was true not only for the Norse, he claims, but also for the rest of Christian-ized Europe, where fish was generally eaten only on fast days. As a result, the Greenland Norse probably starved to death even with an abundant food source at their very doorstep (2005, 268–76, esp. 274). If this theory is true, it should not be surprising that there are no fish mentioned in the entirety of *Aislinge Meic Conglinne,* although references to other sea-related items, such as different types of seaweed, are abundant. Instead, the meats mentioned most often in our text are beef and pork. Diamond would argue that Ireland, like the Greenland Norse and the rest of Christianized Europe, valued cows, pigs, and sheep—livestock that needed to be maintained and tended—as high-status food animals (Diamond 2005, 222–35, 243–47). But fish, particularly trout and salmon, were often referred to in Irish literature. In fact, Finn Mac Cumhaill, the hero of an entire cycle of tales, was depicted as receiving his celebrated poetic powers by eating a special "salmon of knowledge." Cooking the fish for his poet master, Finn accidentally burned his thumb while turning the fish; he stuck his thumb in his mouth and as a result ingested all the knowledge the salmon had to offer. As Joseph Falaky Nagy points out about this episode in *The Wisdom of the Outlaw: The Boyhood Deeds of Finn in Gaelic Narrative Tradition,* the act of cooking and access to otherworldly knowledge are intimately connected in Finn's lore, just as they are in *Aislinge Meic Conglinne:* "By being assigned what at first might appear to be the perfunctory task of cooking the salmon, the 'insignificant' [Finn] is given possibly the most important, most symbolically charged function in the transmission of knowledge from beyond human society to the poet on the riverbank, who is to consume and utilize it on society's behalf. [Finn], a living symbol of transition, is asked to effect the transformation of the salmon from raw to cooked, and of the knowledge it contains from wild and inaccessible to cultural and usable" (1985, 157).

Given the precedent of fish as such an important food, then, it is intriguing that our text does not employ it, symbolically or otherwise.[7] Instead, the food items mentioned most frequently are dairy

---

7. The absence of fish in an anticlerical text such as this one might also lead the reader to speculate about the Christian symbolism of fish; does their absence go beyond the literal to include an absence of the divinity?

products and cuts of meat from cows and pigs, lending credence to Diamond's theory about the use of high-status foods as indicators of culture and civility. The proper consumption of high-status foods reflects the health of the culture, but the refusal or inability to offer those high-status foods illustrates who deserves satire, as a lack of civility threatens the social order.

When Mac Conglinne arrives at the guesthouse of the monks of Cork monastery, social protocol is unobserved: Mac Conglinne waits fruitlessly for someone to wash his feet in clean water, provide him with clean bed linens, build him a fire, give him food, or even notice his existence, all of which were reasonable expectations. Instead, when the monks finally realize that someone is in the guesthouse, they bring him a small amount of raw peat and a cup of whey water. Mac Conglinne has had to wash his own feet in dirty water and wrap himself in verminous blankets, yet the abbot has already criticized him sight unseen. When the monks do bring him his portion, and Mac Conglinne realizes that his conditions are not going to improve, he immediately satirizes the hospitality of the monastery in verse that comments on the poor quality of Cork's soil, as it provides no sustenance, and the substandard quality and quantity of food brought to him. Mac Conglinne answers the rudeness of the monks with (perhaps deserved) rudeness of his own. The text is clear about what is wrong with the Cork monastery at this point: it is shirking its hospitable responsibilities. Mac Conglinne's satire performs its function admirably: it points out through ridicule what is owed to him and other guests by the monastery. The insult may have been directed at him personally, but his response illustrates that the monastery's obligation is not simply to one person but to the codes of hospitality in general.

Satire in early Ireland is generally pointed at an individual, or the individual representative of a larger institution, such as, in this case, a monastery. On a larger scale, though, satire could point out corruption within a larger institution, and in our tale corruption in the medieval Irish church may be linked to the description of the refined food in the tale. Scott James Gwara explains that, for the medieval church, gluttony was simply a preliminary to the greater sin of lust. Cathal certainly qualifies as a glutton, but Gwara asserts that Mac Conglinne is also one and that his ability to cure Cathal's gluttony "by gluttony questions the nature of sin itself" (1988, 71). The church advocated fasting as penance for various sins, and Mac Conglinne, acting as the church's agent, convinces Cathal to fast with him. But when Mac Conglinne restrains and teases Cathal by feeding himself enormous quantities of savory meat, he is replicating the lack of hospitality offered him by the church and using sin to cure sin, tacitly supported by the church. Additionally, the amount of food described in the tale borders on the grotesque, even taking into consideration that much of it is only described and not ingested. The church certainly would have argued against such a gross abundance of food, regardless of its availability. "The repertory of foods rehearsed in the story coincides with that available in the Ireland of the time (no fountains of wine, no stuffed peacocks, no oranges, in short no exotic foods), and that the food fantasy differs from everyday experience not in quality but only in quantity" (Sayers 1994, 8). The food visions recapitulate the dietary regulations prescribed by many monastic rules of the time but exceed them in the amount allowed, thus possibly implying again that the church is too stingy.

Mac Conglinne's subtle criticisms of the church again call attention to his role as intermediary between the church and secular politics. Mac Conglinne covets, but does not yet possess, the role of poet. As a result, Dan Melia argues, Mac Conglinne essentially buys his way into a higher position within the social hierarchy by starting with some seed capital—in this case some bacon and two wheaten cakes—that gives him "alimentary autonomy" in a culture that revolves around food and the expectations of hospitality (2007, 5). He uses the food to buy time and receives in exchange two of his visions; these visions quite literally save his bacon, as they are the impetus for Manchín to send him to Cathal mac Finguine instead of executing him. And Mac Conglinne again uses a version of the vision to rid Cathal mac Finguine of the demon of gluttony. Melia argues that this exchange is an essentially mercantile transaction that has a huge payoff at the end (2007): although his initial investment is bacon and two wheaten cakes, Mac Conglinne parlays it into gifts of livestock, expensive garments, and a not insignificant rise in social status. Food is used throughout our tale as a vehicle, but it is only in conjunction with the power of the spoken word, whether in satiric or in vision form, that food has any role to play at all; without Mac Conglinne's verbal facility and acuity, his ability to convert his visions to poetry, and his understanding of the appropriate use of satire, Cathal mac Finguine would never be saved.

This potent combination can most clearly be seen in Mac Conglinne's initial treatment of Cathal mac Finguine. When Mac Conglinne first meets Cathal mac Finguine, Cathal's shortcomings are immediately clear. Cathal gobbles apples with two hands and does not offer to share any, although he has dozens of companions and retainers with him. Mac Conglinne begins to smack his lips quite loudly, but Cathal does not notice. Cathal notices Mac Conglinne only when the latter begins to grind his teeth against an enormous stone used to test strength and sharpen weapons. The grinding of his teeth is loud enough to penetrate the sound of Cathal's chewing, and he pauses to ask Mac Conglinne what makes him "demented." Mac Conglinne stresses Cathal's noble heritage and the importance of his lineage in his reply, which is fairly standard when addressing the nobility. More important, however, is Mac Conglinne's stress upon Cathal's lack of hospitality. The sign of a good king is his generous nature. If a king is not generous with food, this lack is also a sign that he is not generous with other things, such as gifts or the granting of land and women, and his political reputation will suffer accordingly. Cathal's treatment of food, then, as Mac Conglinne points out, is implicitly tied to his political reputation, and if he is stingy with his food, he makes himself look bad, in front of not only his own people but also people "from distant lands." Although not satirical in itself, Mac Conglinne's damning by faint praise serves the same didactic function as satire, illustrating Cathal's responsibilities to others and the reasonable expectations others have of him.[8] It is to Cathal's advantage that he recognizes this fact, and passes Mac Conglinne an apple, whereupon Mac Conglinne makes a game of seeing how many apples he can win from Cathal before his patience is exhausted.

Transgressive eating symbolizes what is wrong with the culture in our text. As long as people eat normally, all is right in the political, religious, and social realms. But as soon as Cathal tries to eat too much, he effectively harms his kingship and destabilizes the political situation in medieval Ireland. And when Mac Conglinne is offered too little to eat at the monastery, the implication is that the monastery may also be offering too little physically and spiritually to its followers. It is only when Mac Conglinne removes the demon of gluttony that this transgressive behavior stops and order is restored to the society, namely, by reinstituting proper amounts of generosity: Cathal becomes a good king again by showering Mac Conglinne with rewards and averting a famine in his kingdom, and

---

8. There is a category of verse satire called *tamall molta,* or "touch of praise," in which tradition this section would fit, although this part of the text is not in verse but prose (Mercier 1962, 109; Meroney 1950, 204–5; McLaughlin 2008, 52–53).

Manchín, the Cork abbot, becomes a generous representative of his institution, bestowing his hooded cloak on Mac Conglinne. The restitution of normal eating, then, brings about the restitution of the social order. But that restitution cannot happen without the intercession of satire, properly used and applied, to call attention to the defects of the individuals who threaten the social order in the first place.

SATIRE AND CONNECTIONS
TO THE LARGER LITERARY WORLD

The writer of *Aislinge Meic Conglinne* did not restrict himself to the strictly Irish version of satire in his text; he also used general satire, as well as other variants of the genre common to medieval literature on the Continent, such as estates satire, parody, and lampooning. As one example of general satire, we have only to look at the author's use of the Bible within the tale. Cathal mac Finguine ingests the demon of gluttony when he eats bewitched apples sent to him, as he thinks, by his lover Lígach, a motif of temptation and its punishment meant to invoke the story of Adam and Eve. Scott James Gwara convincingly argues that the story has even further uses for *Aislinge Meic Conglinne:* "Since in a Christian hermeneutic [the apple] signifies transgression and sinfulness as well, apple imagery becomes particularly apposite in the context of Cathal's rapacious hunger. Gluttony was commonly linked to original sin, which was itself an act of consumption and an abrogation of restraint in Christian doctrine" (1988, 56). Cathal therefore becomes representative of the fall of humanity, as Gwara goes on to claim. And just as humanity was redeemed by Jesus, so too does Cathal have a savior in Mac Conglinne. Apples play a role here, too: now they are "the beginning of [Cathal's] redemption," as Gregory Darling points out

(2006, 133). Cathal is shamed into sharing apples with Mac Conglinne, a first step toward being socially rehabilitated and consuming appropriate amounts of food, which concludes with Cathal's complete recovery. Although Gwara and Darling both make completely valid analyses, we should not forget that these parallels were also meant to be funny. Through the lightly satirical use of the familiar biblical symbolism, the author of *Aislinge Meic Conglinne* mockingly elevates Cathal to the level of Adam, subject to the wiles of a woman (as he believes) and still capable of bringing about the downfall of an entire population, if not humanity itself. The stakes are not as high as in the biblical tale, but the parallels are unmistakable.

The same is true for Mac Conglinne's mock Passion and Resurrection, suffered at the hands of the Cork monks and abbot. Whereas Jesus has his disciples and a supportive community behind him at all times, Mac Conglinne always operates on his own; Mac Conglinne's relative isolation is one of the major differences in the respective Passions and a notable component of *Aislinge Meic Conglinne* itself.[9] This lack of community first makes itself known when Mac Conglinne arrives at the guesthouse of the Cork monastery, where he waits in vain for adequate hospitality, as discussed above. And whereas Jesus shares himself, quite literally, with his disciples at the Last Supper, in the form of communion, Mac Conglinne is denied both food and community by the monks. Later, when he is granted his request to eat the rations he has brought with him, his Last Supper is remarkable because he chooses to eat alone and to provide for himself, instead of being provided for, as Jesus is. What is being satirized, then, in this lightly blasphemous representation

9. In the H text, Mac Conglinne has one companion who disappears from the narrative just before Mac Conglinne's mock Passion.

of Mac Conglinne as Jesus, is the improper behavior of the community of monks; the implication is that, even if Jesus himself showed up at this monastery, he would receive the same poor treatment as Mac Conglinne, perhaps culminating in a death without any promise of redemption.

If Mac Conglinne is Jesus in this satirical Passion, then Manchín the abbot is Pilate. Manchín happily whips and strips Mac Conglinne, as Pilate does Jesus in most of the evangelists' reports.[10] But Manchín does not exhibit any of Pilate's sympathetic characteristics; indeed, whereas Pilate is forced by the crowd to crucify Jesus, Manchín's own family of monks desires to give Mac Conglinne a respite, which Manchín refuses. Mac Conglinne is finally supported by a community, but that community's desires are trumped by the adamancy of a powerful individual, certainly an echo of medieval Irish life and its social hierarchies. The criticism here is squarely leveled at the amount of power that specific highly placed individuals can arbitrarily wield, when they should be working for the good of their community. The author's familiarity with biblical symbolism is employed as local political commentary, illustrating by negative example the rights and responsibilities of kings and monasteries.

In addition to using the Bible as an influence for his satire, the author of our text also worked within the wider European world of literary allusion. At the time that *Aislinge Meic Conglinne* was written, there was a vigorous satirical movement ongoing in Europe in Latin, by poets who have come to be known as goliards. This extremely loosely affiliated group of poets wrote poems celebrating "wine, women and gambling" and were satirical in their bent, including many "attacks on the establishment" (Adcock 1994, x).

---

10. See Matt. 26:63–66, Mark 14:61–64, and Luke 22:67–71.

One of the most famous of the goliardic poets was Hugh Primas of Orléans and Paris; his poems date from about the 1140s.[11] As a sample of the type of satire that the goliards employed, included below is part of a poem about false hospitality:

My host was my good friend, or so he would profess:
lavish with words, he gave me in actual fact much less.
I shan't reveal his name, should anyone enquire;
but I can say what he was like: he had red hair.
Thinking I'd meet with a most generous reception,
I stepped into a den of trickery and deception. . . .
While I was there, it happened that I consumed one day
some rather strong new wine, and more than was my way.
After the over-sumptuous meal I longed to sink
wearily into bed; I'd had too much to drink.
My cunning host, amused, gave me a sidelong look
and saw me nodding, scarcely able to keep awake.
"To sleep when we're so full," he told me, "isn't wise.
Come on, my guest and friend, let's play three-guinea dice."
Greedily viewing my few coins and meagre purse
he added "If it suits you, why don't you throw first?"
So, rushing headlong to my ruin on the swell
of the feast, I threw the dice: they didn't fall out well.
(Adcock 1994, 2–3)

In the lines quoted here we can see one of the same concerns as in our text: an overwhelming interest in the proper dispensation of

---

11. Edwin Zeydel has argued that this type of Latin secular poetry dates back to the late tenth century, although the earlier poems lack the sophistication and wit of the twelfth-century ones (1966, 14). Therefore, this type of satirical goliardic poetry was certainly contemporaneous with *Aislinge Meic Conglinne*.

hospitality. In this case, the poet does indeed receive ample room and board, but the underlying motivation belies the offered hospitality. Additionally, the beginning lines of the poem accord with one of the legal definitions of satire in early Ireland, innuendo. Hugh Primas does not tell us who his false host is, but hints at who he might be.

The goliards were satirists themselves, but they do not seem to have regularly employed any particular satirical genre to dispense their satire. In the eleventh and twelfth centuries, the obvious option available to them, as it was also used in Latin compositions, was estates satire. Estates satire is perhaps most famously associated with Chaucer's "General Prologue" to *The Canterbury Tales,* but the genre was present centuries earlier. Estates satire has as its aim pointing out the foibles and unpleasant characteristics of the three estates—clergy, nobility, and commoners—of the Middle Ages. *Aislinge Meic Conglinne,* in its criticism of the behavior of the abbot of the monastery of Cork, is satirizing the estate of the clergy; Mac Conglinne also criticizes both Cathal and Pichán, members of the noble estate. Awareness and use of larger satirical traditions being used throughout Europe during the same time illustrate that *Aislinge Meic Conglinne* is not merely an insular text but was influenced by, and perhaps itself influenced, the wider literary world.

A European genre that *Aislinge Meic Conglinne* may have helped give rise to combines the use of satire with a depiction of the fantastic Otherworld, best exemplified by *The Land of Cokaygne* and *Das Schlaraffenland.* The European idea of the Otherworld, whether called Paradise, Valhalla, Elysium, or something else, has general similarities to the Celtic *Tír na nÓg* (Land of Eternal Youth): these conceptualizations of the Otherworld fantasize extraordinary solutions to common problems, such as food shortages, finding a suitable (or better!) mate, lack of mobility within a social hierarchy, and mortality. Tales about the Otherworld, in other words, had existed for hundreds, if not thousands, of years before *Aislinge Meic Conglinne*. So had satirical tales, particularly in the Latin tradition. But *Aislinge Meic Conglinne* might be an early representative of a combination of these motifs, later so well treated in texts such as *The Land of Cokaygne* and *Das Schlaraffenland*. *The Land of Cokaygne* is remarkably similar to *Aislinge Meic Conglinne,* and much briefer. Here, as in *Aislinge Meic Conglinne,*

Al of pasteiis beth the walles,	All of pastry are the walls;
Of fleis, of fisse and rich met,	Of meat, of fish and rich food,
The likfullist that man mai et.	The most savory that man might eat.
Fluren cakes beth the schingles alle	Cakes of flour make all the shingles
Of cherche, cloister, boure and halle,	Of church, cloister, bower and hall.
The pinnes bet fat podinges,	The pinnacles are fat puddings—
Rich met to princez and kinges.	Rich food for princes and kings.
(Lucas 1995, lines 54–60)	(K. Kelly 2009, lines 54–60)[12]

Additionally, the rivers flow with oil, milk, honey, and wine (Lucas 1995, lines 45–46). The earliest date for *The Land of Cokaygne* is approximately 1330 CE, and it goes much further in its satire of the clergy than *Aislinge Meic Conglinne.* In the monasteries within *The Land of Cokaygne,* the monks fly to a nearby convent, swoop down upon the bathing nuns, take them to the abbey, and

---

12. Although Lucas provides a translation with her edition, it is not in verse, which is why I have chosen Kelly's. Kelly's entire text—including the Middle English—is also easily accessible online.

teach them "a prayer with a raised leg up and down" (K. Kelly 2009, 159–66). *The Land of Cokaygne* thus incorporates sexual fantasy into its anticlericalism, but otherwise partakes of the same tradition of satire, the fantastic, and food as *Aislinge Meic Conglinne*. These similarities are hardly surprising if we take into consideration that the earliest copy of *The Land of Cokaygne* comes from a manuscript that was written in Ireland. *The Land of Cokaygne*, in addition to four other poems, is unique to the manuscript. Four of these five unique poems are satirical (Lucas 1995, 9, 22). There is an earlier French version of *The Land of Cokaygne* called *Fabliau de Cocagne*, written in the thirteenth century, that includes descriptions of sumptuous food and clothing, sexual pleasure, a lovely climate, and a fountain of youth, just as in *The Land of Cokaygne*, but this earlier French version lacks the satire against the clergy (ibid., 174). Herman Pleij argues that "Cockaigne must certainly have traveled around Western Europe for centuries before its realization in writing in the few examples we still possess in Old French and Middle Dutch" (1997, 58). The Middle Dutch versions date to the mid-fifteenth and early sixteenth centuries (ibid., 48, 50) and are missing the clerical satire, just as the earlier French versions. At a later point in their transmission history, then, the versions of Cokaygne, across multiple vernaculars and hundreds of years, solidified into satire-free versions that employed several components: "the motifs of eternal idleness, the superabundance of food, and the edible architecture" (ibid., 55). *The Land of Cokaygne*, then, may have been working within an insular tradition of anticlerical satire, possibly derived from the goliards. In fact, there is one goliardic poem that references "abbas Cucaniensis," or the abbot of Cockaigne, who issues a short verse:

I am the abbot of Cockaigne,
  and I take counsel with my drinking companions,

And my persuasion is that of the gambling fraternity,
And if anyone consults me in the tavern at matins,
Come vespers, he'll have lost the shirt off his back:
And being thus fleeced of his raiment will cry–
"Save me! Save me!
What have you done, god-forsaken dice?
Now you've made me sacrifice
All I knew of paradise!"

(ibid., 395)[13]

This poem, part of the *Carmina Burana,* has been dated to the 1160s, later than our text but still a part of the larger European cultural milieu.

Cokaygne has been enormously influential on secular literature and art over the centuries. Later versions of Cokaygne include Schlaraffenland (German), Luilekkerland (Dutch), Lubberland (English) and the Big Rock Candy Mountains (American), spanning the early fifteenth century (Schlaraffenland) to the early twentieth (Harry McClintock's "Big Rock Candy Mountains"). Pleij argues that as tales about Cokaygne wane in the Low Countries, the tales about Schlaraffenland and Luilekkerland increase, but they all involve the same essential components of idleness and abundance of food (ibid., 392). Although there were earlier writers such as Lucian who wrote about an Otherworld filled with fantastic food, and who also wrote satires, *Aislinge Meic Conglinne* is at the forefront of the European tradition of Cokaygne tales, which combine satire and the Otherworld (Ackermann 1944, 32). In this way, *Aislinge Meic Conglinne* is a much more sophisticated text than has previously been

---

13. See also Zeydel 1966, 86–87, for the Latin and an alternative English translation.

recognized, fully conversant with European traditions and perhaps influential in the creation of the later popular Cokaygne tales. And these texts, in their turn, are the direct precursors to later European satirists and parodists such as Rabelais, Swift, Dryden, and Pope, to name but a few. The text is beautifully situated to enable us to learn not just about Ireland in the late eleventh and early twelfth centuries but about the wider world (and the Otherworld) with which it concerns itself.

The Texts, Genre, and Date of *Aislinge Meic Conglinne*

There are two extant manuscripts of the tale: the fifteenth-century *Leabhar Breac,* or "Speckled Book," which resides at the Royal Irish Academy in Dublin, and a sixteenth- to seventeenth-century manuscript, H.3.18, held at Trinity College, Dublin. The *Leabhar Breac* version of the tale, hereafter known as "B," has been studied most often because it has been twice edited. Kenneth Hurlstone Jackson published an edition of B in 1990. Before his edition appeared, the only scholar to have done substantial work on the text was Kuno Meyer, whose editions and translations of both B and "H," as the Trinity College manuscript is known, were published in 1892.[14]

Austin Clarke, the Irish poet and playwright, developed a dramatic version of *Aislinge Meic Conglinne* called *The Son of Learning* in 1927, and it was performed in that year at the Cambridge Festival Theatre, as well as at the Gate Theatre in Dublin in 1930 under the title *The Hungry Demon (The Son of Learning)* (Clarke 2005, 321, 325). Padraic Fallon, another Irish poet and playwright, was influ-

---

14. I follow Meyer's and Jackson's abbreviations for the manuscripts.

enced by Austin Clarke's Verse-Speaking Society, and produced a radio play entitled *The Vision of Mac Conglinne* in 1951, which was produced for broadcast on Radio Éireann, and appeared on BBC Radio and other Continental radio programs (Owens and Radner 1990, 456, 458). In addition to these modern adaptations of the text, a translation was published by Patrick K. Ford in *The Celtic Poets: Songs and Tales from Early Ireland and Wales* in 1999. Other than these versions, the text has not received much attention, either scholarly or popular, but it is an exemplary text in its treatment of many ideas central to medieval life: food, politics, law, poetry, the church, and social status.

Aislinge Meic Conglinne arises out of a long tradition of vision tales in Old Irish, all of which focus on the Otherworld. There are four types of early Irish Otherworld tales: *aislingí, baili, echtrai,* and *immrama*. For the Irish the Otherworld was not a land of the dead but a land of possibility and immortality, where everything a man could ever imagine—which generally entailed variations on beautiful women and incredible foods—was available. There is one other early *aisling* tale, *Aislinge Óenguso*. Óengus has a dream vision of an unbelievably beautiful woman with whom he falls in love. She visits him nightly, but in the meanwhile he wastes away from love for her for nearly a year, until he is able to join her in the Otherworld himself (Shaw 1934). In *aislingí* and *baili* the protagonist has a vision or dream of the Otherworld, without physically going there, whereas in *echtrai* and *immrama* the protagonist actually goes to the Otherworld, often also called the terrestrial or earthly paradise. There is a distinction between these two latter kinds of tales: *echtrai,* or "outings," are more concerned with a description of what happens in the Otherworld, whereas *immrama* consider more valid the process of the journey itself (*immrama* literally means "rowing about") (Mac Mathúna 255–56). *Aislinge*

Meic Conglinne is slightly unusual in its eschewal of any sexually related motivations for a visit to the Otherworld; instead, Mac Conglinne's visions appear only in order to aid Mac Conglinne in curing Cathal mac Finguine, the king of Munster. Also slightly unusual in *Aislinge Meic Conglinne* is the emphasis on food to the exclusion of all else that might be significant about the Otherworld; although many tales mention the food of the Otherworld, they also concentrate on other aspects, such as the beauty and hospitality of the inhabitants, the incredibly sweet music they produce, and the peaceful and harmonious lives they lead.[15]

The manuscripts of B and H mentioned above are later than the tale itself, indicated by several factors. One of the tale's main characters, Cathal mac Finguine, was a historical king who ruled Munster in the early to mid-eighth century CE. This detail alone would

15. There are a number of *echtrai* and *immrama* written during the eighth to tenth centuries, during the Old Irish period, of which the writer of *Aislinge Meic Conglinne* may have been aware. Some of the *echtrai* still extant are: *Echtra Condla* (Oskamp 1974), *The Adventure of Laeghaire Mac Crimhthainn* (Jackson 1942), *Echtra Nerai* (Meyer 1889), and *Serglige Con Culainn* (Dillon 1953). This last tale is not called an *echtra* but fulfills all the same requirements of the genre. The *immrama* still extant are: *Immram Brain* (Mac Mathúna 1985), *The Voyage of Mael Duin* (Stokes 1888a, 1889), *The Voyage of the hUí Corra* (Stokes 1893), and *The Voyage of Snedgus and Mac Riagla* (Stokes 1888b). Additionally, the early *Aislinge Óenguso*, mentioned above, would probably have been known to the composer. Finally, there are also Latin versions of these types of tales written in the ninth century, such as the "Vita Prima S. Brendani" (Plummer 1968a [1910]) and the *Navigatio Sancti Brendani* (Selmer 1989 [1959]), and the later twelfth-century "The Vision of Tnugdal" (Picard and Pontfarcy 1989) illustrates that such vision tales were still popular during the time that *Aislinge Meic Conglinne* was being composed. For an in-depth discussion of *echtrai* and *immrama*, see Séamus Mac Mathúna's *Immram Brain* (1985, 238–85).

not be enough to date the tale as older than the fifteenth century, however. Meyer dates the tale on internal linguistic and historical evidence—which mainly revolves around the system of tithing to the church—to the end of the twelfth century (1974, x). He also contends that there was an earlier version of the tale that no longer exists.[16] Jackson, on the other hand, believes that the tale was composed a century earlier, in the last quarter of the eleventh century for the *Leabhar Breac* manuscript (1990, xxvi).[17]

Dating a text like *Aislinge Meic Conglinne* matters because of its literary influence. As argued above, *Aislinge Meic Conglinne* is working within a wide variety of insular and Continental genre, including estates satire, goliardic verse, and Otherworldly ideas of a land of plenty. Were *Aislinge Meic Conglinne* written in the last quarter of the eleventh century, it would be a precursor for most of these genre, making it a highly influential but barely recognized text. I find it much more likely that *Aislinge Meic Conglinne* was working within these traditions, known to the author, and participating in the wider life of the Continent in the beginning of the twelfth century.

16. Meyer's preface to his edition and translation is remarkably brief. The introduction to his edition was written by Wilhelm Wellner, a structuralist who seeks to prove that the two extant manuscripts actually derive from an older original that no longer exists and that the tale has parallels to many other tales in different cultures (specifically French and German). Meyer also believes that the tale had an older original, which he mentions when discussing the dating of the tale.

17. Jackson's introduction to his edition is thorough, covering the existing manuscripts, the meter of the poems, and the date of the tale. It also includes an analysis of the tale, which takes into account both B and H. His edition also includes an appendix that deals exclusively with Middle Irish and how the language changed from Old Irish; this appendix is based on the Middle Irish texts available to him.

Meyer's rationale for his dating of the text is not particularly convincing: when he was working on *Aislinge Meic Conglinne* and other Middle Irish texts in the 1890s, he was not yet expert enough in the specifics of that language to produce completely accurate dating. He did not even have the tool that linguists rely upon, a grammar of the language (and one still has not been written). He was one of the first scholars doing extensive work on Middle Irish, but had to compile his knowledge based on changes from Old Irish, and then the further changes evinced by Modern Irish. Still, his assessment of the language of *Aislinge Meic Conglinne* is practically nonexistent: "In the absence of any published investigations into the characteristics of the Irish language at different periods, I cannot speak with certainty [about the age of the Vision]. But from a comparison of the language of the *Leabhar Breac* text with that of a fair number of dateable historical poems in the *Book of Leinster* and other early MSS., I have come to the conclusion that the original from which this copy is descended must have been composed about the end of the twelfth century" (1974, x). Meyer here gives no solid linguistic evidence for the dating of the text to the end of the twelfth century. He does not say which poems he is using from the *Book of Leinster,* or the other manuscripts, as comparison.

As for his argument about the tithing system employed by the church, Jackson argues conclusively that this evidence cannot reasonably be considered. Meyer had admitted that the payment of tithes to the church was mentioned earlier than the twelfth century, but asserted that they were "not generally paid in Ireland till the second half of the twelfth century, and then not without much opposition" (ibid.). He mentions the 1152 Synod of Kells as the main impetus behind the collection of tithes. Jackson, however, points out that the *claim* to tithes by the church was in place as early as the seventh century, whether they were actively collected or not, and that this claim is what Mac Conglinne was satirizing (1990, xxv–xxvi).

Jackson, in his introduction and appendix, thoroughly discusses the characteristics of Middle Irish that lead him to believe that the text was composed between 1075 and 1100. First, he begins with the texts that were actually written in the Middle Irish period, which include *Saltair na Rann,* the *Lebor na hUidre, Togal Troí,* the *Passions and Homilies,* the *Book of Leinster,* particularly its version of *Táin Bó Cúailnge,* and *In Cath Catharda* (ibid., xx–xxii). McCone's more recent work on Middle Irish establishes that the most important of these texts for linguistic purposes are *Saltair na Rann,* the *Lebor na hUidre,* and the *Book of Leinster* (1997, 167; 2005, 173). Middle Irish is different from Old Irish in several key ways, such as the demise of the neuter gender in nouns, definite articles, and adjectives; the abbreviation of the definite article; the loss of distinction between the nominative and accusative cases in nouns; and new uses for the independent and infixed pronouns. Verbs, however, are where the changes between Old and Middle Irish are most striking. Old Irish verbs are extremely complicated: they are compound verbs, and they often contain infixed pronouns, which is one of the distinguishing characteristics of the language. In Middle Irish, however, the verb underwent massive simplification: in its structure (that is, the distinction of prototonic and deuterotonic was lost, and most verbs turned into simple weak verbs), in its personal endings, and in the way in which the future and past tenses were created (Jackson 1990, 77–140; McManus n.d.; McCone 1997, 163–240; 2005, 173–218). These examples are just a few of the markers used to identify Middle Irish.

Middle Irish was in use from ca. 900 to 1200 CE, and shifts in the language understandably occurred over those three hundred

years, so Jackson uses *Saltair na Rann*—written in 988—as the early
Middle Irish text against which to judge *Aislinge Meic Conglinne,*
and *Togail Troí* and the *Passions and Homilies* as Middle Irish texts
of what he believes are approximately the same date as *Aislinge Meic
Conglinne;* in other words, the last quarter of the eleventh century.
Jackson summarizes the characteristics of *Aislinge Meic Conglinne*'s
language that lead him to date the text as he does in painstaking
detail: some of his observations are based on prepositional and con-
junction forms that were not used until the Middle Irish period,
and some on verbal forms that changed even further in Middle Irish
after the writing of *Aislinge Meic Conglinne,* when compared to later
texts such as the *Book of Leinster*'s *Táin Bó Cúailnge* (1990, xxiii,
97–104). And while Jackson is nothing but thorough, he uses two
texts—*Togail Troí* and the *Passions and Homilies*—that are not con-
sidered canonical for his terminus ad quem. His arguments would
be more convincing had he used the language in *Lebor na hUidre*
and the *Book of Leinster* more extensively as comparisons. Jackson
notes about the *Passions and Homilies* that they are themselves writ-
ten in different periods of time, and the *Togail Troí* has not been
investigated in almost fifty years, so they should probably no lon-
ger be considered the definers of temporal boundaries (1983, 6–7;
Mac Eoin 1961). Additionally, most of the texts that Jackson uses
as comparisons were thought to be written about 1100 CE, almost
guaranteeing that Jackson would then find the *Aislinge* to be writ-
ten at the same time. But there is nothing to say that it could not
have been written slightly later, in the first quarter of the twelfth
century, for example. His argument that the text was certainly not
written about 1150 as had previously been asserted is entirely valid,
but there is nothing in his arguments to eliminate the possibility
that the text was written anywhere between 1075 and 1125 CE.

Introduction

A Note on the Translation

The basic argument of translation theory is whether one should translate word for word or sense for sense, and the general consensus is that translators must translate sense for sense, as word for word is impossible.[18] Beyond this basic argument, though, translation theory falls, very roughly, into two camps: "domesticating" and "foreignizing." Domesticating a translation requires the translator to familiarize all aspects of the text for the reader, thus making the reader as comfortable as possible when reading the text and not requiring that the reader work to comprehend unfamiliar cultural issues described in the text. A foreignizing translation, on the other hand, demands that the translator keep the source text intact as far as possible, not eliding unfamiliar cultural issues, but confronting the reader with them. Nor should the translator create a translation that is easy for the reader to comprehend. In all ways, the difficulty of what is foreign should be represented, so the reader can begin to become accustomed to a weltanschauung different from his or her own. Friedrich Schleiermacher promotes foreignizing translation in his 1813 essay "On the Different Methods of Translating":

> Either the translator leaves the author in peace as much as possible and moves the reader toward him; or he leaves the reader in peace as much as possible and moves the writer toward him. . . . [I]n the first case the translator is endeavoring, in his work, to compensate

---

18. Even Jerome, the translator of the incredibly influential Vulgate Bible, said that he used sense-for-sense translation: "Indeed, I not only admit, but freely proclaim that in translation [*interpretatione*] from the Greek—except in the case of Sacred Scripture, where the very order of the words is a mystery—I render not word for word, but sense for sense" (2004, 23).

for the reader's inability to understand the original language. He seeks to impart to the reader the same image, the same impression he himself received thanks to his knowledge of the original language of the work as it was written, thus moving the reader to his own position, one in fact foreign to him. (2004, 49)

Schleiermacher advocates for foreignizing translation for several reasons. He claims that a domesticating translation is more of a paraphrase or imitation of the original text, necessitating excisions and rewritings of the original text, than a foreignizing translation, which he sees as a work of art in its own regard. The translator is thus more than a mere interpreter of the material and should instead be seen as an artist in the same way that the original text's author was an artist. Foreignizing translation requires that the "reader is always to remain aware that the author lived in another world and wrote in another tongue" (ibid., 60). Schleiermacher argues that it is impossible to sustain the fiction that the original author wrote just the way the reader of the translation is accustomed to reading her own language: in this particular case, that the unknown author of *Aislinge Meic Conglinne*, a text written approximately nine hundred years ago in a version of the Irish language that is no longer used, wrote anything that could be perfectly comprehensible to an English-speaking and -reading twenty-first-century audience.

Moreover, every language has its own characteristic features, including the rhythms of its prose as well as its poetry, and if the fiction is to be put forth that the author might also have written in the language of the translator, one would have to make him appear in the rhythms of this language, which would disfigure his work even more and limit to a far greater extent the knowledge of his particular character, which the translation was to preserve (ibid., 61).

According to Schleiermacher, then, the translator should do everything in her power to keep a sense of the foreign in the translated text, as an illustration that, for one thing, the world is not univocal and languages are different. Schleiermacher's thinking was enormously influential on such twentieth-century translators and translation theorists as Walter Benjamin, Ezra Pound, Jorge Luis Borges, Antoine Berman, and Kwame Anthony Appiah.

The other side of the coin is domesticating translation, and two of the most famous proponents of this type of translation are Nicolas Perrot D'Ablancourt and John Dryden. Both wrote and translated in the seventeenth century: D'Ablancourt translated Tacitus and Lucian, and Dryden translated many authors, including Ovid and Chaucer. D'Ablancourt began a translation tradition whose products become known as *les belles infidèles,* seen as beautiful but unfaithful (Venuti 2004a, 17). In his preface to the works of Lucian, D'Ablancourt makes the case that Lucian is worth translating even though some of his material was objectionable to his readers:

> One need not find strange, then, my decision to translate this Book, following the example of several learned Persons who have produced Latin Versions, whether of one Dialogue or another; and I am the less blameworthy as I have retrenched what was most obscene and, in some passages, tempered what was too loose. . . . I shall say only that I have left his opinions wholly intact, since otherwise this would not have been a Translation, but I respond to the most intemperate in the Argument or in the Remarks, so that no injury might result. (2004, 35)

In other words, D'Ablancourt bowdlerized the text, removing what was morally objectionable to his readers and calming the rough seas of excess emotion. Dryden, too, when considering his translations of Chaucer, admitted:

> Having observed this redundancy in Chaucer, (as it is an easy mat-
> ter for a man of ordinary parts to find a fault in one of greater,) I
> have not tied myself to a literal translation; but have often omitted
> what I judged unnecessary, or not of dignity enough to appear
> in the company of better thoughts. I have presumed farther in
> some places, and added somewhat of my own where I thought
> my author was deficient, and had not given his thoughts their
> true lustre, for want of words in the beginning of our language.
> (1992, 27)

Both D'Ablancourt and Dryden endeavor, at the least, to make their readers morally comfortable with the authors they are translating and do not make their readers confront what is different about the text, in terms of language, emotions, or cultural beliefs. This approach is extremely different from what Schleiermacher and his followers advise, keeping as much as one can of what is foreign in the translated text. And, as is clear from D'Ablancourt and Dryden, what might be considered foreign refers not only to ways of constructing language but also to cultural matters that may be objectionable to the reader of the translated text.

As a translator, I too have been influenced by Schleiermacher and his followers. I believe that readers should be allowed to experience what is different from and possibly difficult for them. This complexity is a compelling reason to read literature, after all. But Schleiermacher's ideas are idealistic. Having been trained as a post-structuralist and led to believe in the indeterminacy of language—any language—has added yet another level of difficulty to translation. I must consider not only how to translate linguistic, temporal, and cultural differences but also how to replicate the slipperiness inherent in Middle Irish with something similar in Modern English. This dilemma is the partial explanation for such a long introduction, meant to give the reader some grasp of the temporal and cultural differences evidenced in the text.

As for the linguistic differences: Modern Irish is what I would characterize, for lack of a better term, as a passive language. For example, emotional and physical states are described with the use of prepositions: "I am hungry," *tá ocras orm,* literally means "there is hunger on me"; "I like it," *is maith liom é,* literally means "it is good with me"; and "I am in a hurry," *tá fudar fúm,* literally means "there is a flurry under me." Ownership is also described with a preposition: "I have a pen," *tá peann agam,* literally means "there is a pen at me." Direct agency is avoided in the very construction of the language itself. Irish relies on the relative clause and the conditional verb. All of these qualities were true, and even more so, for Middle Irish. Middle Irish also relies on the passive verb, and all these characteristics mean convoluted sentences in which the passive voice and the use of personal pronouns often obscure who is performing the action of the text, making the sentences extremely difficult to parse for the contemporary English reader. And that is just the prose.

Medieval Irish poetry is notoriously even more difficult: poems should begin and end with the same word, or at least the same syllable, a practice known as *dúnad* (Murphy 1961, 43), and the type of meter used determines requirements about alliteration, type of rhyme, and position of rhyme. Unlike English verse, Irish verse regularly uses consonantal rhyme, and the consonants are split into different classes. Consonants can rhyme within their own class, and sometimes with another class. Because Irish has both long and short vowels, vowel length must also be considered when rhyming.

Moreover, like English, Irish has both perfect rhyme—rhyming
within consonantal class or matching vowel lengths—and imperfect
rhyme. And although the position of perfect rhyme often occurs
at the end of the rhyming lines, like English, there are many types
of meter that require, for example, the second and fourth lines to
rhyme perfectly, but the end of line 1 to rhyme with the beginning
or interior of line 2, a type of rhyme called *aicill*. Finally, and per-
haps most important, rhyme can occur only in stressed words (ibid.,
26–45). To take a specific example: the last stanza of the poem that
I have translated as beginning "Brother," on page 11, in which Mac
Conglinne satirizes the hospitality of the monastery, is written in
the *Rannaigecht fhota recomarcach*, generally known as *rannaigecht
bec*, meter (ibid., 53).

Geb-si chucat in n-arán	You take back the bread again,
ima ndernais-[s]iu t' oróit;	Who prayed over it farther,
in chuit-si is mairg do-s-méla;	Who would eat this woe deserves
is iat mo scéla, a scoló[i]c.	That's my story, my brother.

(Jackson 1990, 7)

This meter consists of heptasyllabic lines that end with a disyllable
(notated as 7^2, 7^2, 7^2, 7^2); "*b* and *d* rime, and *ac* consonate with
them. There are at least two internal rimes in each couplet, and
the final word of *c* rimes with a word in the interior of *d*" (Knott
1957, 13–14). Here, *oróit* and *scoló[i]c* are perfect rhymes, because
they both have long *o* vowels, and *c* and *t* are in the same consonant
class. The consonance, or *uaitne*, is found between *arán* and *oróit*
and *scoló[i]c*, where the vowels, although not the same, are long;
the consonance is not perfect, though, because the quality of the
consonants that follow those vowels is not the same (Middle Irish,
like Modern, distinguishes between slender and broad consonants).

There is internal *aicill* rhyme between -*méla* in line c and *scéla* in line d, but there are no other internal rhymes, making this example not quite a perfect *rannaigecht bec*. Finally, for this meter, "two words must alliterate in each line, the final of *d* alliterating with the preceding stressed word" (ibid., 14). In this particular stanza, the first three lines are missing alliteration, but the fourth line, d, fulfills the requirements with *scoló[i]c* and *scéla*.

These strict meter restrictions apply to one stanza of one poem. The first stanza of this particular poem is also in *rannaigecht bec*, but the middle two stanzas are in completely different styles. Several of the poems in this text vary their meter from quatrain to quatrain. I have throughout replicated the metrical requirements of each poem, which no translator has attempted before, and have managed a fair bit of alliteration, but have not always been able to match the rhyme schemes; I hope that this brief example is enough to illustrate why.

To today's English reader, then, this text is beyond strange. My emphasis in the translation aims for foreignizing, but necessarily domesticates some things. As Lawrence Venuti writes in "Translation, Community, Utopia," it is impossible for translators to avoid domesticating: "Translation never communicates in an untroubled fashion because the translator negotiates the linguistic and cultural differences of the foreign text by reducing them and supplying another set of differences, basically domestic, drawn from the receiving language and culture to enable the foreign to be received there" (2004b, 482). Even with the best of intentions, translators are simply not able to sustain a wholly foreignizing mission, because a certain level of domestication cannot be avoided. Again, Venuti argues that "translating is always ideological because it releases a domestic remainder, an inscription of values, beliefs, and representations linked to historical moments and social positions in the receiving culture. In serving domestic interests, a translation provides an ideological resolution for the linguistic and cultural differences of the foreign text" (ibid., 498). This translation does have a decidedly domestic interest: it is intended for the use of American undergraduates, who as a general population do not have a great deal of experience with other languages or medieval literature. I want the translation to be recognizably foreign, for the audience to have to struggle a bit, but I have limited that effort to mainly cultural issues. In a move that may cause some disquiet among my colleagues in Celtic studies, who are traditionally conservative linguistically, I have not translated the Middle Irish in all its glorious complexity. I have, for the most part, removed the passive voice, and I have not employed archaisms, as Kuno Meyer did. This translation is geared toward a general audience, one interested in, but not necessarily familiar with, medieval Ireland and its customs.

The bracketed numbers in the margins of my translated text refer to the corresponding lines in Kenneth Hurlstone Jackson's edition of the Middle Irish text (1990), with the goal of facilitating classroom use by both instructors and students.

AISLINGE MEIC CONGLINNE
The Vision of Mac Conglinne

Every work of literary skill, including this one, should satisfy four things, that is, a place, a person, a time, and a motive for creation.[1] In this work, the place was great Cork in Munster,[2] and the person was Anér Mac Conglinne of the Eóganachta of Glendamain.[3] The

1. This beginning is a traditional formulaic opening sequence that "often occurs in religious and historical works from at least the 8th century on" (Jackson 1990, 45). But to use such a learned literary phrase to introduce a work of satire is clearly a send-up of the literary establishment.

2. Munster is the southernmost province of Ireland. Cork is one of the primary cities of Munster. Medieval Ireland was divided into provinces, such as Munster and Ulster, but it was also divided into the Northern Half and the Southern Half. As Joep Leerssen explains, "All territorial and clannish relationships had stratified into a system which pivoted on a customary rivalry between Leath Mogha and Leath Chuinn, the 'Southern' and the 'Northern' Halves of Ireland, the competing domains of the Munster kings and their neighbours to the North. . . . Leath Mogha [the Southern Half] is named after . . . the Munster king Mugh Nuadhat" (1994, 17–18). There are references to the Southern Half throughout the text, privileging the importance of Munster and Cork against the attempted hegemony of the Uí Néill dynasty in Ulster. See the introduction for further information.

3. Anér/Aníer is an extremely rare name, and Jackson posits that the "etymology" of Anéra given below (no refusal) is invented (1990, 45). Mac Conglinne means "son of the hound of the glen." The Eóganachta are descended from Mugh

1

work was created in the time of Cathal mac Finguine,[4] son of Cú cen Gairm or son of Cú cen Máthair. The motive for creating the work was to expel the demon of gluttony living in Cathal mac Finguine's throat.[5]

[11] Cathal mac Finguine was a good king who ruled Munster; he was a great warrior prince. He was this kind of warrior: greedy as a dog and hungry as a horse. Satan, namely a demon of gluttony in his gullet, consumed Cathal's food with him. A pig, an ox, and a large bullock, with sixty loaves of pure wheat, a vat of new ale, and thirty hen's eggs were what he started with, not to mention his between-meal snacks, until his main meal was ready for him. As to the main meal, there was no way to account for it at all.

[20] Cathal mac Finguine had a demon of gluttony in his throat because Lígach, daughter of Maeldúin, king of Ailech, was in love with him (even though she'd never laid eyes on him).[6] Lígach was sister to Fergal, son of Maeldúin, who was another king of Ailech, and at that time he was the defender of Ireland against Cathal mac Finguine, as is evident from the contention of the two hags who dueled in quatrains in Achad Úr[7]:

Nuadhat through his grandson Eógan Mór, and are thus one of the primary septs of the Southern Half, Leath Mogha (Leerssen 1994, 18).

4. According to Jackson, Cathal, son of Finguine, ruled Munster from 721 to 742 CE and was from a different dynasty of the Eóganachta than Mac Conglinne (1990, 45).

5. The "demon of gluttony" in Irish is *lon cráis*. Cathal most likely has a tape-worm or an eating disorder.

6. Ailech or Oilech is in present-day County Donegal and was one of the seats of the kings of Ulster (Meyer 1974, 130).

7. Achad Úr is currently known as Freshford, in County Kilkenny (Jackson 1990, 46).

Down from the North [27]
Comes Maeldúin's son, rock-hopping,
Brink of Barrow,
He will not stay when cow-stealing.

He will! He will! (said the southern hag)
When he bolts he'll show gratitude;
By my father,
If he meets Cathal, no pilfering.[8]

Lígach, daughter of Maeldúin, sent seeds and apples and many [35]
other delicacies to Cathal mac Finguine for his love and affection.
Fergal, the son of Maeldúin, heard about that, and summoned his
sister. He offered her a blessing for telling him the truth and a curse
if she lied. His sister told him, because whatever love and affection
she had for Cathal mac Finguine, she was afraid of her brother's
curse. So she told him the whole true story.

Fergal told her to send the apples to himself. He summoned a [43]
scholar and promised him great rewards if he would bewitch those
tasty things, to destroy Cathal mac Finguine. So the scholar threw
spells and enchantments on the delicious treats and delivered them

---

8. In this poem, the northern hag is Fergal's advocate, and the southern hag
is Cathal's. They each claim victory for their patron if ever they meet and a conflict
ensues. Cattle raiding was an illegal yet popular pastime, and the hags refer to this
practice in their poem.

This poem is of a type called *ollbairdne*, which has a meter of 4^1, 8^3, 4^2, 8^3. In
other words, the first line has four syllables and ends in a monosyllable, the second
line has eight syllables and ends in a three-syllable word, and so forth. Lines b and
d rhyme, and there is *aicill* between lines c and d; additionally, there is alliteration
in each line (Murphy 1961, 51, 61). I have replicated the meter (except that my last
line is hypermetrical), and have included some alliteration.

to Fergal, who sent them with messengers to Cathal mac Finguine. They begged him by the eight universal things, namely sun and moon, dew and sea, heaven and earth, and day and night, to eat those apples, brought to him because of the love and affection of Lígach, daughter of Maeldúin.[9]

[53]   Cathal ate the apples, and magical creatures were made in his stomach. And those wee creatures then gathered together in the belly of one of them, and so the demon of gluttony was formed. So the reason that a demon of gluttony was created in the gut of Cathal mac Finguine was to destroy the men of Munster in eighteen months, and it is likely it would have destroyed Ireland altogether in another six months.

There were eight people in Armagh at that time about whom these songs were sung:

[62]   I have heard of eight tonight
in Armagh, after midnight;
I swear by my many deeds
Their nicknames not savory.

Son of Two Crafts is Comgán,
Well-known to follow hunting.
Crítán also Rustaing's son,
His grave sets women giggling.

Dark One of Two Tribes, a pure
name for son of Stelene,
Black Raven; fair Hag of Beare,
Rough One from Oaks, Mac Samán.

9. Swearing by these natural constants is common in early Ireland; so is the breaking of any such vow, which is then punished (Jackson 1990, 47).

4

Don't deny Mac Con Glinne [74]
from banks of Bann sweet-singing.
The Littles, man and wife, were
dad and mom to the "dead-man."

My king, king of heaven vast,
Leads soldiers to battle gains,
No dying, Mary's fine son,
I have heard of a huddle.[10]

---

10. This poem describes several odd characters, about whom little or nothing is known. The poem is perhaps a way of establishing Mac Conglinne's credentials as a poet by linking him with the other characters, although most of these characters seem to be jesters or buffoons rather than serious poets; it may also help establish his link to the North, by highlighting Armagh. Comgán Mac Dá Cherda (Son of Two Skills) was a legendary Munster character who was also a prophet, mentally unstable, and a wild man of the woods. Crítan mac Rustaing had the dubious distinction of inducing every woman who saw his grave to fart or give a loud, silly laugh; he was probably some sort of jester. Dub Dá Thuath mac Steléne, the Dark One of the Two Tribes, has been identified by Thomas Owen Clancy as Mac Teléne, "a Munster character in an Old Irish tale in the Yellow Book of Lecan" (1992, 81). Donn-Fhiach, Black Raven, is unidentified. The Caillech Bérre is the Hag of Beare (in the southwest of Counties Kerry and Cork) about whom much has been written. Garb Daire (Rough One of the Oak Grove), like Comgán, is known as a Wild Man of the Woods. Finally, Becán and Becnait (the little one and his wee wife) are listed as Marbán's parents: Marbán (little corpse) was most probably a hermit who lived in the woods. Except for Donn-Fhiach, these figures all have associations with the wild, with poetry, and with prophecy. See Jackson 1990, 47–49.

The poem is written in *deibide* meter, stanzas composed of four lines of seven syllables each; a rhymes with b, and c rhymes with d. *Deibide* is the most common of the poetic meters. This particular version is *deibide scáilte*, which means "scattered" *deibide*. It is so called because the syllable count for the final word of the line varies from line to line instead of being regular (Murphy 1961, 28n1, 29, 65ff). In this particular poem, the meter is: $7^2, 7^2, 7^1, 7^3; 7^2, 7^2, 7^1, 7^2; 7^1, 7^3, 7^1, 7^2; 7^2, 7^3, 7^1, 7^2;$

[83]   One of these eight, then, namely Anér Mac Conglinne, was a wonderful scholar with heaps of knowledge. He was called Anér because he would satirize or praise anyone. It was a fitting name, because there was never before or after him anyone whose satire or praise was more of a burden. That's why he was called Anér, or "Nonrefusal," because there was no denying him.

[89]   A great desire came upon the scholar to give up his studies and to pursue poetry. To spend his life studying was wretched,[11] and he considered where he should make his first poetic circuit. He decided to go to Cathal mac Finguine, who was then on a royal circuit of Iveagh in Munster.[12] The scholar had heard of the amount and quality of every kind of dairy product to be had there, and he was greedy, craving dairy.

[97]   This idea came into the scholar's mind one Friday evening in Roscommon, where he was studying. After that, he sold the little

---

$7^1, 7^1, 7^1, 7^2$. I have reproduced the syllable count, and have also used alliteration, not necessarily in only the stressed words.

11. There is an echo of Ecclesiastes 4 here.

12. Royal circuits were undertaken for a number of purposes: they asserted the king's territorial boundaries, they established the king's presence among his people, and they allowed the king to collect various forms of food-rent, including an annual feast held by a client for his lord and his retinue between New Year's Day and Shrovetide (F. Kelly 1988, 29–30). The practice probably originated from monastic *cúarta,* wherein the abbot of a monastery would make a circuit of the monastery's lands with the monastery's relics and collect rent and offer protection to the people. See also Bitel 1990, 166; and Jaski 2000, 105. As Jackson points out, the tradition of the *cuairt fhilidechta,* or "the professional visitation by a high-class qualified poet to a succession of noble patrons," is used ironically, as Mac Conglinne has no retinue with him, which a high-status, respected, and established poet would (1990, 49).

Iveagh is a territory in southwest County Cork (Meyer 1974, 134).

property he had for two loaves of wheat bread and a piece of old bacon with a stripe down its back. These things he put in his book bag. And that night he fashioned a pair of pointy brown shoes from leather folded seven times.

He got up early the next morning. He put on his tunic and [104] pulled it up over his buttocks, and then wrapped his white cloak in folds around himself. He pinned an iron brooch through the cloak. He strapped on his book bag and gripped his well-balanced staff in his right hand. He went around the graveyard clockwise. He said good-bye to his teacher, who put the gospels around him.[13]

He set off on his journey, and traveled through Connacht, into [112] Slieve Aughty, to Limerick, to Carn Fheradaig, Berna-Trí-Carpat, into Slieve Caín, into the land of the Fir-Féni, which is today called Fermoy, across Móin Mór, until he rested, just before Vespers, in the guesthouse of Cork. He had traveled all the way from Roscommon to Cork on that one Saturday.[14]

He found the guesthouse standing wide open. That day had [118] three seasons in it, namely wind and snow and rain in through the door. There was not a piece of thatch or a speck of ash, but the wind swept it through the other door, under the beds and benches and along the walls of the royal guesthouse. The blanket of the guesthouse was bundled up on the bed, full of fleas and lice. And no surprise, as it was never aired out in the sun during the day nor shaken out at night because it was in almost constant use. The bathtub of

---

13. A copy of the gospels was hung around Mac Conglinne's neck as a lucky amulet.

14. Mac Conglinne has walked an incredible 120 miles in one day. The guesthouse is part of the monastery at Cork. Canonical hours are kept at monasteries. Vespers is held at sunset and has specific Psalms (109–47, not including 118) assigned to it.

the guesthouse still had dirty water from the night before in it, and the warming stones were by the doorjamb.

[128]   The scholar found no one there to greet him and wash his feet.[15] So he took off his sandals and washed his own feet in the dirty water. He rinsed his sandals in that water as well. He hung his own book bag on his staff, and leaned them against the wall, and he hung up his own shoes. He picked up the blanket and wrapped it around his legs. But, honestly, as many as are the sands of the sea or sparks in a fire or dews on a May morning or stars in the heavens were the lice and fleas nibbling at him, which disgusted him and made him weary, and no one came to enquire about him or see if he needed anything.[16]

[137]   He took down his book bag, pulled out his psalter, and began singing the Psalms. The wise men and books of Cork say that the sound of the scholar's voice was heard for a thousand feet outside the city chanting the Psalms, through their spiritual mysteries, in hymns of praise, annals, in sections, with pauses and changes from note to note, in decades, with paternosters and canticles and hymns at the end of every fifty Psalms.[17] It seemed to every man in Cork,

---

15. In John 13, Jesus washes the feet of his disciples at the Last Supper. By performing such a humble task himself, Jesus makes the point that his apostles should also be humble. One can also imagine that after a long day of walking on medieval "roads" one would need to wash one's feet, and that the offer to do so would be a staple of hospitality. The monastery's guesthouse, then, in providing only dirty water, and no humble monk to wash Mac Conglinne's feet, fails to show proper humility or hospitality.

16. See the introduction for the importance of hospitality in medieval Ireland; essentially, the monastery's guesthouse does everything wrong.

17. Psalms are an important component of Vespers (see note 14). According to Meyer's *Old Irish Treatise on the Psalter,* diapsalms separate out what misreadings have joined together and sympsalms join together what misreadings have separated.

moreover, that the sounds were coming from the house next door. Mac Conglinne's poor treatment resulted from original sin, from his ancestral sin, and from his own bad luck, so that he was kept without drink, food, or bathing, until after everyone in Cork went to bed.

After he went to bed, Manchín,[18] abbot of Cork, said: "Son, are there guests with us tonight?" [149]

"There are not," said the servant.

But another servant said, "I saw someone crossing the green boldly and impatiently a little while before Vespers."

"It's preferable to know who he is," said Manchín, "and take him his food."

Mac Conglinne had had no desire to go back again to get his food, especially as it was a bad night.

Mac Conglinne's provisions were brought out, and this is the meal brought to him: a little bowl of oatmeal made of whey water from the church, two embers of fire in the middle of a bundle of oat husks, and two sods of raw peat. The servant came to the door of the guesthouse and was seized with fear and terror at the wide-open, darkened building. He didn't know whether someone was there or not. As he put his foot over the threshold, he called: "Is there anyone here?" [157]

It also seems that sympsalms used a number of voices and diapsalms only one (1894, 30–31). Decades are groups of ten Psalms sung together. Mac Conglinne's volume in singing the Psalms parodies various saints' lives, in which the saint can be heard singing Psalms up to one-half or one full mile away. See in particular Adomnán of Iona's *Life of St. Columba* (1995, 141).

18. Manchín means "little monk." This designation continues the text's introduction of the Cork monastery and those individuals associated with it as worthy of little respect.

"There is," said Mac Conglinne.

"It violates the *gessa* to prepare this house for just one man."[19]

"If the *gessa* have ever been violated," said Mac Conglinne, "it was tonight, for they were fated to be broken and broken by me."

"Get up," said the servant, "and eat your meal."

"I swear," said he, "because I have been kept waiting until now, I will not get up until I know what you have brought." The servant put the two embers in the middle of the bundle of oat husks on the hearth, and added to it another bundle of wisps pulled from the straw mattress of the bed. He arranged the two sods of raw peat around the bundle, blew on the embers, lit the bundle, and showed Mac Conglinne his dinner.

And Mac Conglinne said:

[175]
"Brother," said Mac Conglinne,
"Why not contend in poesy?
You make stanzas on brown-bread,
I'll sing about the chutney.

Cork has sweet-sounding bells, although
Its sand wanting,
Its soil sandy,
In food it is lacking.

I won't eat 'til Kingdom-Come
Unless a famine happens,
The meager Cork oat-porridge,
Cork's gruel, tiny platters.

19. "A *geis* [pl. *geisi* also *gessa*] is a supernatural injunction or 'tabu' which forbids the performance of certain acts by an individual or group. The term may also be used of the prohibited action itself" (F. Kelly 1988, 20).

10

You take back the bread again,
Who prayed over it farther,
Who would eat this woe deserves
That's my story, my brother."[20]

The servant memorized the stanzas, for he was a clever one.

They brought the food back where Manchín was and repeated [193]
the stanzas to the abbot.

"Well now," said Manchín, "bad language is the delight of a
boy. Little boys will sing those kinds of verses, unless the one who
made them is punished."

"What are you going to do, then?" said the gillie.[21]

Manchín said, "I will go to the one who made these stanzas and
strip off all his clothing, and ply staffs and whips on him until his

---

20. The meter of this poem varies from quatrain to quatrain. The first verse is
rannaigecht chetharchubaid gairit recomarcach, which has a syllabic count of 3^2, 7^2, 7^2,
7^2. As in all *rannaigecht* meters, b and d should rhyme perfectly. There should also be
consonance between a and c, and *aicill* rhyme between c and d (although in this stanza
the consonance is imperfect and there is no *aicill*). There should also be alliteration in
every line (Murphy 1961, 55). The second verse is 8^2, 4^2, 4^2, 6^2, which is a variation on
dechnad cummaisc (ibid., 50). Perfect rhyme is expected between b and d, consonance
between a and c, and *aicill* rhyme between c and d. This particular verse has *aicill* but
no consonances, and instead of rhyme between b and d, it has rhyme between a and d.
There is also alliteration in b and c. *Ae Freislige* is the meter of the third verse, with a syl-
labic count of 7^3, 7^2, 7^3, 7^2 (ibid., 62). The same requirements for rhyme, consonance,
and alliteration apply to this verse as to the previous two stanzas discussed. Finally,
verse 4 is *rannaigecht bec,* with a syllabic count of 7^2, 7^2, 7^2, 7^2 (ibid., 53). Again, the
requirements for rhyme, consonance, and alliteration are the same as the previous three
quatrains. I have kept the syllabic count and included as much alliteration as possible,
and sight, if not full, b and d rhymes. Additionally, I have replicated *dúnad.*

21. Gillie is the anglicized term for *gilla,* which means a servant, apprentice,
or slave.

11

flesh parts and bursts and separates from his bones—but without breaking his bones. I will dunk him in the river Lee and give him a good soak in its muddy waters, and then return him naked to the guesthouse." (And remember there was nothing in the house except the blanket, in which lice and fleas were as plentiful as dews in May. He sleeps there that night in the most wretched and darkest state he was ever in.) "Lock him in the house until morning, so that he cannot escape, until my judgment, along with the counsel of the monks of Cork, can be processed against him tomorrow, before the Lord and Saint Barra, whom I serve.[22] There is no other sentence but his hanging tomorrow, to save face for me, and for the honor of Saint Barra and the church." All that was done, and then it was that his own original sin and everyday sin arose against Mac Conglinne. All his clothing was stripped off, and scourges and horsewhips sang on him. He was put into the Lee and given more than his fill of its muddy waters. He spent the night locked in the guesthouse.

[217] Manchín rose early the next morning and collected the monks of Cork together near him at the guesthouse. It was opened for them, and they rested on the benches and couches in the house.

"Well, wretch," began Manchín, "you did not do justice to the church's honor last night."

"The people of the church did no better," answered Mac Conglinne, "to leave me without food, and myself such a small party."

"You were not without food, even if you only got a small loaf or a drop of whey-water in the church. There are three things that should not be complained about in the church, that is, fresh fruit, new ale, and Saturday night's supper. For even though there is very

22. Saint Barra, also known as Saint Finnbarr, is the patron saint of Cork. His *floruit* is mid-sixth century to early seventh century. See Ó Riain 1994.

12

little that's received on Saturday night, what's most important in the morning is Psalm singing, bell ringing, preaching, celebrating mass, and feeding the poor. A fast on Saturday night finds a feast on Sunday or Sunday night. You began complaining much too early."

"I confess, then," answered Mac Conglinne. "We have been [232] made obedient, and the retaliation was excessive."

"But I swear before the Creator and Barra," said Manchín, "that you will not satirize again. Take him away with you, so that he may be hanged on the open green for the honor of Barra, the church, and myself."

"Cleric," said Mac Conglinne, "do not hang me, but let a fitting, fair judgment be passed on me, which is better than hanging me." Then they proceeded to pass judgment on Mac Conglinne. Manchín began to prosecute against him. Then every man of the monks of Cork, in order of rank, took his turn prosecuting Mac Conglinne. Though they had a lot of wisdom and knowledge and learning, they could not find any legal passage for which he could be hanged.

Then they brought him anyway, illegally, to a green on the south [244] side of Cork. He said, "Do me a favor, Manchín and monks of Cork!"

"Is it to spare you, then?" asked Manchín.

"I'm not asking that," answered Mac Conglinne, "though I'd be happy enough if that came of it."

"Speak," said Manchín.

"I will not speak," said Mac Conglinne, "until I have guarantees for it." Pledges, strong bonds, and sureties were imposed upon the monks of Cork for the fulfillment of Mac Conglinne's request, and he bound them with his pledges.[23]

---

23. See F. Kelly 1988, 158–76, for further discussion of these legal concepts. Contracts (usually oral), pledges, and sureties were the backbone of the early Irish legal system. Pledges were "an object of value delivered by its owner for a fixed

"Now say what you want," said Manchín.

"I ask," said Anér, "to eat the piece of the Host that is in my book bag before I die, because it isn't proper to take a trip without going to communion. Bring my book bag to me." It is brought to him, and he opened it and took out of it the wheaten loaves and the piece of old bacon and cut off a tenth of each cake and a tenth off the piece of bacon, appropriately and fairly.

"Here are your taxes, monks of Cork," said Mac Conglinne, "and if we knew anyone who was more deserving or poorer, we would give him these tithes, instead."[24]

[262]   All the paupers there rose up, when they saw the tithes, and held out their hands. And Mac Conglinne scanned them and said, "Honest to God," he said, "I don't know whether any one of you needs these tithes more than I do myself. Not one of you had a greater journey than my own, yesterday, from Roscommon to Cork. I did not eat a mouthful or drink a drop after I got here, I had nothing on my journey, and I did not get the respect due to a rightful guest after I got here. Instead, I found nothing but massive insults, you

---

period into the custody of another" (F. Kelly 1988, 164). They were a type of collateral to ensure the completion of the oral contract. Similarly, there were several different kinds of sureties; some incurred financial liability in the form of collateral, but others simply verbally reinforced the value of the contract. Mac Conglinne goes to extraordinary legal lengths simply to receive a last meal; this conduct gently mocks the legal system.

24. The medieval Irish church expected tithes from its followers in the amount of 10 percent. As Hughes points out, this amount relates not only to first fruits of the harvest but also to livestock and humans. "The first-born son was given to the church to receive an ecclesiastical education: he inherited his share of the family land on his father's death and farmed it as a *sóer-manach* of the church. After ten sons had been born, another son with his inheritance was set aside for the church" (1966, 140). See also Bieler 1963, 166–69.

curs, you robbers, you shitty dogs, you monks of Cork! My clothes were stripped off me, scourges and horsewhips sang on me, and I was dunked in the Lee. There was no fair play given to me, only absolute injustice. So help me God," said Mac Conglinne, "I will not be accused by the devil, when I'm down below, of giving these tithes to you, when they were not deserved." The first mouthful he ate was the taxes themselves, and then he consumed the rest of his meal, both loaves with the piece of old bacon. He lifted up his hands and gave thanks to the Lord.

"Now take me to the river," said Mac Conglinne. He is brought [279] to the Lee, with men to bind and secure him. When they reached the well called Bithlán (Always Full), he took off his fine white cloak and laid it out on the ground. He threw himself down on his back onto the cloak, on top of his book bag for further support. He put his finger through the ring of his penannular brooch, and dipped the point of his brooch over his shoulder into the well. And when the water flowed down the point of the brooch, he put it over his mouth, and so he drank. The monks who guarded him and held him in bondage grew tired.

"Turnabout is fair play, you dogs and thieves, you monks of [288] Cork!" gloated Mac Conglinne. "When I was in my monastic cell, I used to hoard any scraps of food that came my way for five or six days; then I would eat it all in one night, and drink my fill of water afterward. That would keep me going for several days, without having anything else and not a bother on me. I ate enough just now to last three or four days, and another few days doing penance, and another several days drinking water, because I have pledges on my hands. I swear to God and Saint Finnbarr," said Mac Conglinne, "that, high or low, none of the monks of Cork will leave where they are, but they will all die on a single night, Manchín ahead of everyone else, to hell and damnation. I am certain of heaven and will be in the presence of God, of whom there is no end or decay."

[301]   That invective was told to Cork's monks; they called a quick council and decided to bless Mac Conglinne only if he went to his hanging with humility for God; otherwise, nine people would surround and guard him until he died where he was, and then they would hang him afterward. They told Mac Conglinne their decision. "That's for the dogs," said Mac Conglinne—whether he meant that it was a decision made by dogs or a decision for the dogs, no one can say —"but whatever happens, we will go in humility, as our master, Jesus Christ, went to his Passion." He rose up then and surrendered himself to the monks of Cork; by then it was almost the end of Vespers.

"A favor, Manchín!" begged the monks of Cork.

"Oh my God, what favor?" said Manchín.

"To put off hanging that wretch until morning. We have not rung the bells, nor celebrated Mass, nor preached, nor made the Offering. The poor have not been fed, and do not let all Sunday pass by without feeding our own selves. Give us a respite for him until the morning?"

"I vow," said Manchín, "no delay shall be given, but the day of his sin will be the day of his punishment."

[319]   More's the pity! In that same hour, Mac Conglinne is taken to Foxes' Wood, with people guarding him. An ax is put in his hand, and he cut his own passion tree and carried it on his back to the green of Cork. He plants the tree in the ground himself. It was past Vespers, and they have no other plan except to hang him then and there.

"A request, Manchín and monks of Cork," begged Mac Conglinne.

"By my word," said Manchín, "you will get no favors from us."

"I do not ask you to grant me mercy, for, even if I asked, it would not be granted to me of your own free will, you dogs, you robbers, you curs' caca, you ignorant louts, or, to be more specific,

16

you cunning, clumsy, cringing, chapfallen cowl wearers of Cork! But I want my fill of fatty, juicy food, and good sweet intoxicating drinks, and a lightweight, beautiful thin suit of clothes that will protect me and keep me dry, that will keep out the cold and the heat, and I want a fortnight's-worthy feast before I die."

"I swear to you," replied Manchín, "that you will not get that. However, it is the end of the day, and it is Sunday; moreover, the community begs a respite for you. But your scant clothing will be taken off you, and you will be bound to that pillar stone over there, as a taste of what you'll get tomorrow for your main punishment." So that was done—they stripped off his remaining clothing and bound him with ropes and cords to the pillar stone.

Then the monks turned toward home, and Manchín went to the [342] abbot's house. They fed the poor and the guests, and ate something themselves. They let the scholar fast, though, who was sent from the Lord God to save Cathal mac Finguine, the men of Munster, and the whole Southern Half[25] at that. He was not given true justice. He was there until midnight and then an angel of the Lord came to him on the pillar stone and began to give him a vision. When the angel was on the pillar, it was too hot for him; when the angel moved to a ridge in the green, though, it was tolerable. (Thus the "Angel's Ridge" in the green of Cork, that was never a morning without dew.)[26] The angel left him at the end of the night. Mac Conglinne

25. The Southern Half is known in Irish as Leath Mogha, after the Munster king Mugh Nuadhat. See also note 2 and introduction.

26. *Dindsenchas* is the onomastics of place-names in Ireland. *Dindsenchas* often contains legendary material: "Such legends purport to explain the origin of certain place-names by connecting them to events" within the text (Ó hUiginn 1992, 44). There are many examples of *dindsenchas* within this text, and it is a common feature of all medieval Irish texts.

17

composed a little poetic introduction of his own, that was suitable to relate the vision that had been shown to him; he concentrated only on the introduction to his vision until morning.

[357]   The assembly bell was struck by the monks of Cork early the next morning. They all came directly to the pillar stone.

"Well, wretch," said Manchín, "how are you today?"

"Fine," he replied, "if you let me tell you one little thing, that a vision appeared to me last night. Oh, and, if you give me a respite, I will tell you the vision."

"My word," said Manchín, "if the seed of Adam were obedient to me, they would not give you a respite for even a day and a night. I certainly won't."

"By our word," said the community of monks, "like it or not, he will be given a delay so he can tell his vision. Then you can do what you will with him."

Then Mac Conglinne traced Manchín's pedigree up to Adam through a genealogy of food:

[370]   "Blessings on us, cleric,
Famed pillar of wisdom,
Son of Honey-Tummy,
Mac Drippings, Lard's sonny,

Mac Oatmeal, mac Gruel,
Son of ripe fruit, clustered,
Son of cream, thick, silky,
Mac Buttermilk, mac Custard.

Son of Beer, drink perfect,
Son of pleasing Bragget,[27]

27. Bragget is honey and ale fermented together.

18

Son of Leek, so green-tailed,   [380]
Son of Bacon, mac Butter,

Son of well-stuffed Sausage,
Son of Milk, fresh, wholesome,
Son of Nuts, mac Produce,
Son of Grease, mac Gravy,

Mac Lard, son of Kidney,
Son of Ribs, mac Shoulder,
Son of well-cooked Sausage,
Mac Haunch, son of Porridge.

Son of Butt, mac Cheek-Meat,
Son of speckled Sausage,
Mac Gobful, mac Slurping,
Son of Back, mac Belly,

Son of Whey, thin, cloudy,
Son of Cheese yet unpressed,
Mac Fish of Inber Indsén,
Son of curds, mac Soft-Cheese,

Mac Mead, son of Port-Wine,
Son of Meat, mac Pale-Ale,
Son of Wheat, hard, hearty,
Son of Tripe, mac Stomach,

Son of Gruel, stunning,
Made out of pure Sheep's-Milk,
Son of Stew-meat tendered,
Hot, steam wisps like cornsilk.

[406]
Son of Oatmeal, tufty,
Son of Oatbran, gorgeous,
Son of Gruel, streaming
Around purple berries.

Son of tender Cabbage,
Son of soft, white Belly,
Son of Nuts, so ample,
Abel's son, mac Adam.

Fine your good food descent,
Sweet to tongue as honey,
Of pace firm and steady,
Helped by your staff pointy."[28]

[419]
"That doesn't hurt me, Mac Conglinne," said Manchín. "You think nothing of insulting me and the church when you compose a genealogy of food to commemorate me, such as has not been created for any person before and will not be made again until Doomsday."

28. This genealogy is a spoof on the genealogies of their patrons habitually composed by medieval Irish poets. These genealogies are meant to be laudatory, and occasionally go all the way back to Adam; here, Mac Conglinne mocks the tradition by composing a genealogy of food.

This poem is in the *rinnard* meter, composed of lines of six syllables per line, with a disyllabic word at the end of each line. B and d rhyme with each other (Murphy 1961, 64). There should be alliteration between the last word of a and the first stressed word of b, *aicill* between c and d, and alliteration between the last word of a stanza and the first stressed word of the next stanza (Jackson 1990, xvi). I have replicated the syllabic pattern and occasional rhyme schemes and alliteration. I am twice hypermetrical.

"It is no slander at all, cleric," answered Mac Conglinne, "but a vision that was given to me last night. That was its introduction. The vision is not inappropriate, and if I am given a delay and a respite, I will tell you all of it." And Manchín repeated that no respite would be given him. But Mac Conglinne began to tell his vision anyway, and it is said that what follows here is what the angel revealed to him:

> "Vision to me revealèd,   [430]
> Revelation marvelous,
> I tell to you all.
> Made of lard, a coracle
> At port on Lake Newest-Milk
> On the smooth world's sea.
>
> We went in the man-of-war
> And took the path daringly
> Over the rough waves;
> We pulled ourselves—stroke/stroke/stroke—
> Over the sea expansive
> And stirred up the carrageen,
> Honey-colored sand.
>
> We reached a fort wonderful
> With ramparts all custardy
> On the lake's far shore;
> Fresh butter, steps' construction,
> The stone rampart wheaten-white,
> Palisade of pork.
>
> In a pleasant position
> Was the house, strong, substantial.

[451]   And then I went in
Through the door of meat-jerky,
The threshold of dried-bannock,
The walls of soft cheese.

Pillars of cheese barnyardy
And broad beams all bacony
Alternately spread;
Jolly joists of heavy-cream
Bright rafters of cottage-cheese—
They support the house.

Just behind, a wine-wellspring,
Beer, bragget in riversrun,
Tasty each full pool.
A malt sea for ale-brewing,
At a whey-well's boundary
Flows over the floor.

Lake of cabbage succulent
Under fat crust congealèd
'Tween it and the sea.
Butter fences bordering
Beneath lard crest bright-mantled
Were the outside wall.

Rows of fragrant apple-trees
A great orchard, pink-blossomed,
'Tween it and the hill.
A spot with tall vegetables,
Leeks and carrots, upstanding
In back of the house.

22

Smart men inside, generous, [480]
Young and red-haired, flourishing,
Basking at the fire.
Seven torcs[29] and amulets
Of cheese and of chitterlings
Hung at each man's throat.

I then saw their overlord
In his corned-beef overcoat
Near his noble wife.
I saw too the head-waiter
At the cauldron's cooking-spit,
Flesh-fork down his back.

Good Cathal mac Finguine,
Happy he for troubadour
To sing dining tales.
An hour's pleasant performance
And telling it delightful,
The ship rowing roundabout
In Lake New-Milk's sea."[30]

29. Torcs are usually collars or necklaces (although they can also be bracelets, arm rings, and finger rings) made of precious metals such as bronze, silver, and gold. They were traditionally worn by the Celts and the Gauls.

30. This poem is highly unusual. Instead of being arranged in quatrains, the poet has used a six-line stanza. The meter is organized around two triplets: the first two lines are heptasyllabic and conclude with a three-syllable word, and the final line has five syllables, of which the final is monosyllabic (7^3, 7^3, 5^1, 7^3, 7^3, 5^1). This structure is a variety of a meter called *eochraid* (Murphy 1961, 79). There are extra lines (or extralong lines) in verses 2 and 11. Only c and f rhyme, and there is no *aicill*, consonance, or internal rhyme. There is alliteration throughout. I have replicated the meter and some alliteration.

He related his entire vision then, before the monks of Cork, until the end—but this is not its end—and the divine grace of the vision was revealed to Manchín.

[502] "Good, wretch," said Manchín, "go seek Cathal mac Finguine and tell him this vision, for it was revealed to me last night that the evil in Cathal will be cured through that vision."

"What reward will be given me for that?" asked Mac Conglinne.

"Isn't it a great enough reward," replied Manchín, "to let you have your body and your soul?"

"I don't care about that, although they should be given. The windows of heaven are open to me, and all the righteous from Adam and his son Abel, to those righteous ones who go to heaven this very moment, are chanting choral songs, awaiting my soul, until I get to heaven. The nine grades of heaven, including cherubim and seraphim, are waiting to welcome my soul. It's all the same to me if Cathal mac Finguine, the men of Munster, and the Southern Half, the monks of Cork and Manchín himself (especially him), die and go to hell in the same night, as I myself will be in the unity of the Father, the Son, and the Holy Spirit."

[518] "What reward do you want?" asked the monks of Cork.

"I'm not asking for much," replied Mac Conglinne, "just the small, hooded cloak the clergy of the Southern Half were refused, and that they fasted about on the same night: Manchín's cloak."[31]

31. Ecclesiastical vestments are symbolic and intricate. In this case, it is possible that Manchín's small, hooded cloak is a type of cope and is also a symbol of his abbatial office. Before a strict diocesan structure was established in Ireland—in 1152 at the Synod of Kells—abbots wielded the majority of ecclesiastical power. Still, as Jackson points out, "neither text [B or H] gives the slightest indication of why this cowl [or cloak] was regarded as such a valuable object" (1990, xxxv).

"That might not be much to you," interjected Manchín, "but it is to me." He added, "I give my word before God and Barra, that if all the land of Cork and its monastic lands were mine, it would be easier to do without that property than without that small, hooded cloak."

"You'll be sorry if you don't give the cloak," said the community of monks, "because rescuing Cathal and the Southern Half is better than that cloak."

"I will give it then, so," said Manchín, "but I never have and never will again grant a favor more troublesome to me. I will give it into the hands of the bishop of Cork, for him to deliver to the scholar if he helps Cathal mac Finguine." Then it was given into the bishop of Cork's custody, and the monks of Cork delivered the small, hooded cloak, and it was left in the bishop's hands.

"Go now and seek Cathal!" commanded Manchín. [533]

"Where *is* Cathal?" asked Mac Conglinne.

"Not difficult," replied Manchín, "in the house of Pichán, son of Mael Find, king of Iveagh, at Dún Coba on the border between Iveagh and Corcu Loígde; find him there tonight." Then Mac Conglinne went hastily, boldly, impatiently. He hitched up his five-pleated cloak, and fastened it around his shoulders; he tied his shirt up over the bulges of his buttocks, and dressed like that strode quickly across the green on his way to the house of Pichán, son of Mael Find, of Dún Coba, on the border of Iveagh and Corcu Loígde. And he walked swiftly toward the fort. When he arrived at the specific assembly hall where the group was convening, he put on an unseemly hooded cloak and garment; the upper parts got shorter and shorter and the lower parts longer and longer. In this getup he began clowning around for the host of people who were in the king's hall, doing things which were *not* suitable for a person like him: satirizing and farting and singing poems of the higher poets.

25

It was said that never before nor ever again was there one as famous in the craft of satire.

[551]   As he was performing his feats in Pichán's house, Pichán said, as an aside, "Though you are very funny, son of learning, I am not made happy by it."

"Why are you blue?" asked Mac Conglinne.

"Don't you know, scholar," replied Pichán, "that Cathal mac Fin-guine arrives here tonight with the nobility of Munster, and though the great host of Munster is a bother to me, more difficult by far is Cathal himself. His appetizers are bad enough, to say nothing of the first course, but he is most vexatious of all in his main course. Three things are demanded for the main course: a bushel of oatmeal por-ridge, a bushel of crab apples, and a bushel of fine bread."

[562]   "What will you give me," asked Mac Conglinne, "if I keep him away from you from now until the same time tomorrow, and if he does not retaliate against yourself or your *túath*?"[32]

"I would give you a gold armband and a Welsh horse," said Pichán.

"By God, you will have to do more than that!" said Mac Conglinne.

"I will also give you a white sheep for every house and every sheepfold from Carn to Cork," said Pichán.

---

32. "The term *túath* is variously translated as 'people,' 'laity,' 'tribe,' 'ter-ritory' or 'petty kingdom,' depending on its context. . . . The early Irish lawyers regard the *túath* as the basic socio-political unit of their time. . . . The territory of a *túath* could be marked by grave-mounds, by ogam-stones . . . and by uncultivated strips of land or natural boundaries such as rivers or lakes. Scholars have estimate [*sic*] the size of an average *túath* to 15 to 25 km across. The number of people in a *túath* depended on its sizes and resources, but as an average of [*sic*] about 3000 has been proposed" (Jaski 2000, 38).

"I will accept that," replied Mac Conglinne, "on the condition that kings, hospitallers, poets, and satirists are pledged to me as guarantors for the delivery of my complete dues. The kings are to enforce the rightful fees due me, and rich hospitallers are to sustain me with food, ale, and other necessaries while I'm enforcing the payment. If I am cheated out of my dues, then I demand poets to satirize and blame them, satirists to spread the satires abroad, and then sing them against you and your family and your entire people, unless my rightful dues are paid me."[33] And he bound his guarantors so.

Cathal mac Finguine came with the hosts and the cavalry of [577] the men of Munster, and they sat around on benches, couches, and beds. They let gentle marriageable girls wash their feet and wait on them, the entire multitude. But not one of Cathal mac Finguine's two shoelaces had been loosened, or his shoes removed, before he was stuffing his mouth, with both hands, with the apples that were on a tablecloth in front of him. Mac Conglinne was there on the other side of the room, and he began to smack his lips, but Cathal did not notice him. Mac Conglinne leaped up like one possessed by a devil and boldly and impatiently strode with a warlike pace across

33. In early Ireland, there were two main categories of poet: the *fili* and the *bard*. The *fili* is the higher in status and has seven separate grades, the highest of which is the *ollam*. There are also separate grades for the *bard,* but the sources differ about the precise number (F. Kelly 1988, 46–47; Breatnach 1987). In this instance, it seems that Mac Conglinne is asking for both kinds of poets, *filid* to compose the technically difficult satires and *baird* to recite the satires. Legally, Mac Conglinne is requesting an outrageous fee for his services. Pichán's first offer is completely reasonable, and his second one, accepted by Mac Conglinne, is excessive. No king would have stood surety for such a bargain; not only is it immoderate, but to make such an agreement with someone of Mac Conglinne's lower status would have been beneath their notice.

the king's house. And there was a huge block used to test warriors' strength into which spears and rivets were usually thrust for practice and against which spearheads and sword edges were often sharpened. That stone slab had been a warrior's grave marker. Mac Conglinne lifted it onto his back and took it back to the place he was before, on the couch. He thrust the upper part of it into his mouth, rested the other end on his knee, and began to grind his teeth against the stone. The learned men, elders, and the books of Cork all say that there was no one close to the fort, inside or outside, who could not hear his teeth against the rock, smooth as it was.

[596]   Even Cathal noticed this. "What makes you demented, son of learning?" he asked.

"Two things," answered Mac Conglinne, "Cathal, truly beautiful son of Finguine, high-king of the great Southern Half of Ireland, chief defender of Ireland against the descendants of Conn of the Hundred Battles, a man chosen by God, a noble, well-born hero of the fierce Eóganachta of Glendamain, by his paternal heritage: it grieves me to see him eat anything alone. And if people from distant lands were here requesting favors or boons, they would scoff if my mouth was not munching at the same time as yours."

[606]   "That's true," said Cathal, and gave him one apple, and shoveled another two or three into his own mouth. During the year and a half that the demon of gluttony lived in the throat of Cathal mac Finguine, he had never done one such act of kindness as giving the crab apple to Mac Conglinne who had to argue for it strongly.

"Two things are better than one in learning," said Mac Conglinne. Cathal flung him another apple. "The number of the Trinity," said Mac Conglinne. Cathal gave him one. "The four books of the Gospels, according to the teachings of Christ." Cathal bestows an apple on him. "The five books of Moses according to the teaching of the Old Testament." Cathal tosses him one.

28

"The first numeral article that is reckoned by and consists of its [615] own parts and divisions, or the number six—because its half is three and its third is two. Give me the sixth!" Like a shot, Cathal throws an apple at him. "The seven things that were foretold of your God on earth, that is, his conception, his birth, his baptism, etc." Cathal gives him one. "The eight beatitudes of the Gospels, great king of royal judgments!" Cathal hurls one at him. "The nine grades of Heaven, royal champion of the world!" Cathal bestows one on him. "The tenth grade is here on earth, defender of the province!" Cathal pitches him an apple. "The incomplete number of apostles after sin." Cathal produces one. "The complete number of apostles after sin even though there was betrayal!" Cathal grants him an apple. "The acme of acmes and the perfect number, Christ with his apostles."[34]

34. This section is a clear parody of medieval Irish clerical learning, with its emphasis on numerology.

The five books of Moses are the Pentateuch: Genesis, Exodus, Leviticus, Numbers, and Deuteronomy.

The seven things that were prophesied about Jesus are also found in the *Leabhar Breac,* but actually number eight: the Conception, the Birth, the Crucifixion, the Entombment, the Resurrection, the Ascension, the seat on the right hand of God, and the Last Judgment. There is a variant of the *Leabhar Breac,* which gives seven: the Birth, Baptism, Crucifixion, Entombment, Resurrection, Ascension, and Descent for the Last Judgment. *Aislinge Meic Conglinne* seems to have mixed the two lists (Jackson 1990, 59).

The eight beatitudes of the gospels are Matt. 5:3–10.

The nine grades of Heaven are the Nine Orders of Angels.

The tenth order, of Earth, seems to be humanity: "Medieval angelology regarded Mankind as having been created to fill the gap caused by the Fall" (ibid.).

The final three numbers, 11, 12, and 13, refer to Jesus and his apostles. The sin mentioned is Judas's betrayal of Jesus.

"That's it!" protested Cathal, "by Saint Barra, you will eat *me* if you go any further!" Cathal flung the tablecloth with the apples at him, and there was no nook or cranny, floor or sitting surface, that the apples didn't roll into, and if they weren't nearer to Mac Conglinne than anyone else, they were farther away from Cathal. Fury seized Cathal. One eye leaped into his head so far that a pet heron could not have pulled it out. The other eye swelled until it was as big as a full-grown hen's egg, flopping onto his face, and he pressed his back against the side of the king's house until he left not a house post, rafter, wattling, bundle of thatch, or pillar in its place; then he settled down in his seat.[35]

"Behave yourself, king," said Mac Conglinne. "Do not curse me, and do not deprive me of heaven!"

"What did you do that for, son of learning?" asked Cathal.

35. Cathal is here being likened to the famous Irish warrior Cú Chulainn, who was subject to "distortions" or "warp spasms" in which his eyes do exactly what is described here of Cathal. See Kinsella's translation of *Táin Bó Cúailnge, The Táin*, (1969, 150–53). Cathal's destruction of Pichán's house is a reference to "Bricriu's Feast" from *Lebor na hUidre* (The Book of the Dun Cow). In this tale, Cú Chulainn lifts the house of his host, Bricriu, so high that "the stars were visible beneath the wall," so that his wife can enter the building with her retinue of fifty women. He puts the house back down, but it is hopelessly askew and lopsided. Cú Chulainn attempts to correct his mistake but fails. "Then his *ríastarthae* [warp spasm, distortion] came over him: a drop of blood appeared at the tip of each hair, and he drew his hair into his head, so that, from above, his jet black locks appeared to have been cropped with scissors; he turned like a mill wheel, and he stretched himself out until a warrior's foot could fit between each pair of ribs. His power and energy returned to him, and he lifted the house and reset it so that it was as straight as it had been before" (Gantz 1981a, 229–30). Ultimately, this motif may be a comment on the transformative power of anger.

"It was natural," replied Mac Conglinne. "I had a fierce encounter with the monks of Cork last night who brought a complaint against me. That's why I did this to you."

"Ah, go on, Mac Conglinne," replied Cathal. "By the monastery at Emly, if it were my custom to kill sons of learning . . . you'd know better than to have come here, or you would never leave."

Now, he used to swear by the monastery at Emly[36] because he [644] used to get his fill of fine bread there. He'd be there, in his smooth brownish cloak, with his hard, straight-bladed sword in his left hand, snacking in each monastic cell in the place. One day he went into a certain student's cell and found plenty of scraps. He looked over the food. The scholar looked over the page before him. When he finished the page he was reading, he stuck out his tongue to turn the page. "Why did you do that, scholar?" asked Cathal.

"I have good reason," he replied. "I was summoned to go fighting with a host-in-arms to the edge of the world (or so it felt). They gave us a burned, ashy crust of bread, smoky and more than day-old, so that there was nothing nutritious left. There was no morsel of bacon, or butter or other meat, and no drink of any sort except muddy water from the pond, so that I was deprived of my strength and vigor, because of the hosting!"[37]

"Alas," said the son of Finguine, that is, Cathal, "by Saint Barra, while I am alive, not one cleric comes fighting with me from now

---

36. Meyer states—based on W. M. Hennessy's translation of 1873—that Emly is the village of Emly in County Tipperary (1974, 241).

37. The frequent use of the noun *host* or *hosting* in this section refers not to the Host that the priest offers at communion, nor to a host who offers hospitality, but to the military sense of the term. A hosting means a military expedition, and a host-in-arms are the soldiers one takes on a hosting.

on." And until that time, the clerics of Ireland had gone soldiering with the kings of Ireland, but he was the first ever to exempt the clergy from military service.[38] Then he left favors and blessings on the pilgrims of Emly as well as an abundance of fine bread. He left even more in the southwestern part, for he used to get his fill there. This is a digression, though.

[666]   "By your kingship, your sovereignty, and in the name of service owed you, grant me a small favor before I die," implored Mac Conglinne. Pichán was summoned into the house.

"That student there asks a favor from me," said Cathal.

"Grant it," said Pichán.

"I will, then," said Cathal. "What do you want?"

"I won't say without pledges for its fulfillment."

"They will be given," said Cathal.

"Your sovereign word on it?" asked Mac Conglinne.

"I give you my word; now name your request," he said.

"Right," said Mac Conglinne, "this is it. I had a huge quarrel last night with the monks of Cork, and they all put a curse on me. It is that which caused this misunderstanding between you and me. So fast with me tonight on God, since we are kinsmen by ancestry, to liberate me from the curse of the Cork monks.[39] That is my request."

38. This apocryphal story purportedly details the exemption of clerics from military service; see Jackson 1990, 60. Hughes avers that Áed, overking of the Northern Half of Ireland, exempted the clergy from military service at the urging of Fothad of the Canon in 804, approximately sixty years after Cathal's purported reign (1966, 191–92).

39. In medieval Irish law it was not uncommon to fast against someone of a higher rank to pressure that person into giving justice. Essentially, fasting against someone meant going on a hunger strike, perhaps on that person's doorstep, and

"Don't say that, son of learning!" begged Cathal. "I'll give you [680]
a cow from every courtyard in Munster, an ounce of silver from
every tenant, a cloak from every church, and a steward to collect it
all, while you yourself feast in my company when he's out collect-
ing the fines. Hang it all," said Cathal, "I would rather that you
had everything in Munster, west to east and south to north, than I
spend a night without food."

"And *I'll* be hanged," retorted Mac Conglinne, "you already
gave your sovereign word, and a king of Cashel can not go back on
his word! If everything in the entire Southern Half of the country
were given to me, I would not take it. Moreover, chief hero and
royal champion of Europe, I have good reason why I cannot accept
your bribes; my own wealth is in nothing but heaven, or earth, or
learning and poetry. Not only that—saving the best for last—but I
will go to endless, infinite hell unless you rescue me from the Cork
monks' malediction."

"I will do that, then," moaned Cathal, "but a thing more
repugnant to us has never before transpired, nor ever will again,
until Doomsday." Cathal fasted with him that night, as did every-
one else there. The student settled down into a trundle bed beside
the doorjamb, and the house was secured.

When he was lying there at the end of the night, Pichán mac [698]
Moíle Finde arose.

"Why does Pichán get up now?" asked Mac Conglinne.

---

both plaintiff and defendant had to participate in the fast, or the defendant (the
person of higher rank) had to pay double fines. It was not a fast to death, but (most
commentators believe) from sundown to sunrise, thus missing only one meal a day.
Mac Conglinne takes this concept to absurd levels by fasting against God. See F.
Kelly 1988, 182; and Jackson 1990, xxxv–vi.

"To make food for these people," said Pichán, "and it would be better for the place if it were ready since yesterday."

"It is not time to do that," said Mac Conglinne. "We fasted last night, so we will have preaching first thing in the morning." And so they waited until morning. Regardless of how many they were, not one of them went outside or even popped out of bed until it was time to get up in the morning. Then Mac Conglinne himself got up and opened the house. He washed his hands, got his book bag, pulled out his psalter, and began preaching to the troops. The historians, elders, and books of Cork all say that there was neither noble nor commoner who did not let loose three floods of tears while listening to the scholar's preaching. When the sermon was ended, prayers were offered up for the king, that he might have a long life and that Munster would be prosperous for the duration of his reign. Moreover, prayers were offered up for the land and the people and the province, as was usual at the end of a sermon.

[715]   "Well," said Mac Conglinne, "how are things with you today?"

"I swear to God," replied Cathal, "I have never been closer to death before, and won't be again until the end of days."

"It figures you're in a bad way," said Mac Conglinne, "what with the demon blighting you with his magic and devastating you for eighteen months now, and you did not fast a day or night on your own. Now, though, you have fasted with a miserable, wretched insignificant person like me."

"What's the good of that, student?" asked Cathal.

"That's not hard to say. Last night, you were the only one who fasted with me, but tonight everyone will fast, as many as there are of us, and you yourself will also fast to get some help from God."

"Don't say that, son of learning!" Cathal burst out. "The first night was hard, but the second will be seven times harder!"

34

"Don't *you* say that," said Mac Conglinne, "but have the courage to do it." Cathal fasted then with his people from that point until the end of the night.

Then Mac Conglinne got up. "Is Pichán asleep?" he asked.   [729]

"I'll tell you the truth," replied Pichán. "If Cathal were to remain as he is until the brink of Doom, I will not sleep, eat, smile, nor laugh."

"Get up, then," ordered Mac Conglinne, and he demanded bacon fat, tender corned beef, plenty of mutton, honey in its comb, and English salt in a gorgeous, highly polished dish of white silver, along with four good, straight spits of white hazel to cook the food on. What he demanded was fetched, and he put enormous chops on the spits. He put a linen apron around him and a flat linen hat on top of his head, and kindled a handsome, square fire of ash wood with four sections, without smoke, fumes, or sparks. He planted a spit over each section of the fire, and he was as swift around the spits and fire as is a doe with her first fawn, or a roe deer, or a swallow, or the bleak spring wind in the middle of March. He rubbed the honey and the salt into one piece after the other. And as huge as the pieces on the fire were, not one of the four steaks dripped enough to quench the spark of a candle, but they absorbed their own juices into their very core.

It had been shown to Pichán that the reason the scholar had   [749]
come was to save Cathal. When the meat was done, Mac Conglinne commanded, "Bring me ropes and cords!"

"What for?" asked Pichán, and that was a question by conscience (or a rhetorical question), because it had been explained to him before. That is where the old saying "a question by conscience" comes from.[40] Ropes and cords were brought to Mac Conglinne,

40. This "old saying" is unclear. Jackson has an explanation that is also unclear to me (1990, 61).

the strongest ones the warriors had. They laid hands on Cathal and bound him to the wall of the king's house. Then Mac Conglinne came and spent a long time securing the cords with hooks and clasps. And when he had finished, he went in with the four spits held high on his back, his loose white cloak flowing behind him, to the place where Cathal was. He planted the spits by the bench just in front of Cathal and settled himself cross-legged in his seat. He took a knife from his belt and cut a mouthful from the chop nearest him. He dipped it in the honey that was in that silver-white dish.

"This is its beginning instead of a male beast," said Mac Conglinne, and put the morsel into his own mouth. And from then on this proverb persisted.[41] He cut another tidbit from the chops and dipped it in honey and put it past Cathal's mouth into his own.

"Carve some for us, son of learning!" begged Cathal.

"I will," replied Mac Conglinne. He cut a morsel from the chop nearest to him and dipped it in the honey as before and then waved it under Cathal's nose before putting it into his own mouth.

[772]   "How long is that going to last, student?" asked Cathal.

"Not long now. Except that, until now, you have eaten such an excessive amount of outstanding food that I myself will consume the little bit here now, and what's left will be 'food out of your mouth.'" (And that's another proverb.)[42] Cathal howled and roared and ordered the death of the scholar. But it wasn't done.

"Well, Cathal," said Mac Conglinne, "a vision came to me, and I have heard you are a good interpreter of visions."

"I swear to God," replied Cathal, "that even if I could interpret all humanity's visions, I would *not* interpret yours."

41. This traditional saying is unidentified.
42. Here is yet another unclear proverb.

"Suit yourself," said Mac Conglinne. "But I swear that even without your interpretation, I will tell it to you." He began to tell him his vision, all the while putting two or three bites at a time past Cathal's mouth into his own.

"Last night I had a vision   [785]
I went out with two or three
and saw a bright house, well-stocked,
overflowing with good food.

I saw the Lake Newest-Milk,
'Mid a shining plain,
I saw a house, diligent
Thatched with butter pats.

When round it I circuited
To get a good look
Fresh from the pot sausages:
These its thatch-rods were.

The doorposts were of soft custard
The floor of butter and curds
Couches made of splendid suet,
and shields of pliant pressed cheese.

The men strapped into those shield-straps
Were delicious smooth cream cheese;
Engaged not in a Gael's killing;
Each man there had butter spears.

Full of stew a giant cauldron
(I thought I could handle it)

37

[807]   boiled, leafy, brown soup of cabbage,
a huge cup brimful of milk.

Bacon house with forty rafters
Tripe roof-wattles keep clans safe
Every food pleasant to people—
It seemed to me all was there."

Last night[43]

And he continued:

[815]   "A vision last night I beheld
A spell lovely,
Shown me was a mighty power:
Erin's kingship.

I saw the branched, tree-filled courtyard,
Bacon stockade
Ramparts of grain, fine-ground, knobbly,
And pressed cheeses.

43. This poem has no proper *dúnad,* and so the poet has included the beginning of the first line here at the end of the poem as a reminder, perhaps. See Murphy 1961, 43–45.

    This poem is not standard in its rhyme scheme or meter. Verse 1 is heptasyllabic; a and c finish with a disyllable, while b and d conclude with a monosyllable. There is rhyme between b and d, and *aicill* between c and d. This section is loose *rannaigecht mór* (Murphy 1961, 52). Verses 2 and 3 are 7^3, 5^1, 7^3, 5^1, where b and d rhyme. There is very little alliteration, and no internal rhyme or consonance. These stanzas are loose *cró cummaisc etir chasbairdne agus lethrannaigecht* (ibid., 61). Finally, verses 4–7 are 8^2, 7^1, 8^2, 7^1. This meter is called *sétnad,* and again, b and d rhyme. There is often *aicill* between c and d, and a is tied to b by either *aicill* or alliteration between the lines (ibid., 49–50, 54). I have replicated the meter for all these quatrains, but not the rhyme, and not always the alliteration.

The most flavorful pig chitlins   [823]
Made tripe benches,
Pleasant the rafters and pillars
Made from sausage.

Wonderful vision that appeared
By my fireside
Butter game-board with its chessmen,
Smooth, capped, mitred.

God bless the words I affirm
Just right revel!
Once I got to Mount Butter
Servants sent, my wants to attend."[44]

Though it was a hard penalty to Cathal to be two days and a   [837]
night without food, an even greater agony was the recounting of
these plentiful and exotic foods—and none of them for him. Then
Mac Conglinne began a fable:

Last night when I was lying in my cozy, well-made bed, with
its gilt posts and bronze rails, I heard a voice near me, saying,
"Arise, Mac Conglinne, you wretch!" And I did not answer it.
Why would I? My bed was so comfortable, my body so at ease,
and myself so deeply asleep. Then the voice said again:

---

44. As with the last poem, this poem is of varying meter. The first four verses
are meant to be very loose *snédbairdne,* which has a meter of 8^2, 4^2, 8^2, 4^2, where b
and d rhyme. There should be alliteration throughout and *aicill* between c and d
(Murphy 1961, 51). The last verse is quite strange, as it is 7^2, 4^2, 7^2, 8^2. It could still
be hypometric *snédbairdne,* with a hypermetric final line. I have chosen to replicate
the meter as it appears in the text, with some occasional alliteration, but no rhyme.

"Beware, watch out, Mac Conglinne, or the gravy will drown you!" That is, have caution so meat juices don't drown you. I got up early the next morning, and I went to the well to wash my hands. I saw this enormous specter coming toward me.

"Well, then," he said to me.

"Well, indeed," I replied to him.

"Well, now, wretch," said the specter, "I warned you last night about drowning in gravy. But truly, warning you was like:

[854]
    "a warning to one already marked for death,
    making excuses to a beggar,
    a rock falling on a tree,
    whispering to the deaf,
    an inheritance to one who's depressed,
    putting a spell on a hurdle,
    charcoal tied with a willow wand,
    beating an oak tree with your fists,
    trying to suck honey from the roots of a yew,
    begging for butter in a dog's den,
    consuming peppercorns,
    searching for wool on a goat,
    an arrow shot at a stone pillar,
    preventing a mare from farting,
    keeping a bawdy woman from being randy,
    water at the bottom of a sieve,
    trusting a tied-up dog,
    salt on rushes,
    buying a woman after you've slept with her,
    a secret told to a thoughtless woman,
    hoping for wisdom from a fool,
    exalting slaves,
    alcohol given to idiots,
    giving guidance to kings,

a body without a head,
a head without a body,
a nun ringing bells,
an impostor in the bishop's chair,
a kingdom without a king,
rowing a boat without a rudder,
carrying grain in a basket full of holes,
spilled milk,
housekeeping without a woman,
berries on a hide,
visions of Judgment Day to sinners,
defamation for an insult,
restoring without delivering,
sowing seed in bad land,
providing for a lascivious woman,
serving a bad lord,
an informal contract,
a lopsided measurement,
going against judgment,
violating the Gospels,
teaching the Anti-Christ: that's what warning you about
     your diet was like, Mac Conglinne!"[45]

"Hell!" said Mac Conglinne. "That's a harsh scolding!"   [875]
"How do you figure?" asked the specter.
"That's not hard to say," replied Mac Conglinne. "I don't
know where you came from, or where you're going, or anything
at all about you, to question you or be able to know you again."

---

45. This entire list is a catalog of useless or futile actions, as Jackson terms it
(1990, 62).

"That's easily told," replied the specter. "My name is Buaran-nach mac Elcaib Essamain, that is, Diarrhea Sufferer, son of Fearless Potty-Mouth from the Fairy Mound of Eating, Sídh Longthe."

[891]   "I suppose," said Mac Conglinne, "that if that's who you are, you must know a great many tales, and, more than that, you must know stories of food and of eating. Do you know any?"

"I know plenty," replied the specter, "but even if I do, it would not be lucky for anyone to hear them who was powerless to equal them in eating."

"How is that?" asked Mac Conglinne.

"That's not hard to tell you," replied the specter, "that is, unless he had a very broad, long and lengthy, square belly that was five hands high, in which he could find room for twenty-seven eatings and seven drinkings—with enough drink for nine men in each of them—and for the seven chewings and the nine snacks: food for a hundred being in each of those eatings and drinkings and swallowings and snackings respectively."

"Because I know I do not have that belly," said Mac Con-glinne, "give me advice, for you have made me hungry."

"I will," said the specter. "Get up and go to the retreat from which I have come, the hideaway of the Fáithliaig or Witch Doctor, and you will find there the cure for your appetite for all the foods that your gluttony and your heart desire. A place where your teeth will be well employed on the great quantity of the marvelous and varied foods that we have talked about; where your hunger will disappear and your tongue will tingle; a place where your mouth will be full of fine drink and choice dainties, eating and consuming every tasty, sweet, and smooth food your body craves—without feeling guilty! But you must go to the Fáithliaig and to Becnat Bélaide, Little Juicy One, daughter of Mac Baetáin Brass-Longthig, Horny Hugely-Gluttonous, the wife of the Fáithliaig.

[904]   "The day you arrive at the fort will be the day that the Tent of Suet will be set up around them, on a small, wheat-filled field,

42

with the Two Fatties, Sausage, and the good lad of Little Food Pot wearing his lard hood. You will be happy the day you arrive at the fort, Mac Conglinne," said the specter, "because that will be the day that the chiefs of the Tribe of Food will be summoned there."

"And what are their names?" asked Mac Conglinne.

"That's easy," replied the specter. "There is Little Sloe, son of Smooth Juicy Bacon; Cake, son of Fruity Dried Meat; Empty-Sides, son of Sausage; Little Milky, son of Little Milky; Big Biceps, son of Leather-Head, and young Lard-Adorer, son of Haunch of Mature Bacon."

"And what is your own name if I may ask?"

"That's not hard," said the specter:

"Little Wheatie MacMilky   [919]
Moist Bacon's male-offspring
Is my own name;
Honeyed sweet Mousse
The man's name who
Totes my bag.

Leg of Mutton
Is my dog's name,
Does fine deeds.
Suet my wife
Lovingly laughs
Over kale tops.

Sweet Curds my daughter
'Round hearth hustles
Fine her feats.
Corned Beef my son:
Conceals his cloak
The biggest bum.

[937]   Vat O'Cream
Is my wife's serving maid's name
At day's prime
She sailed across Lake New Milk.

My horse Beef-Lard
Soft, moist bacon
Studs a herd;
From loads protects
His cheese saddle
On his back.

When a packhorse
Of bright soft-cheese
Is let behind,
Swift he runs.
Hard fat for reins
Meat on rib-bones
Best of shapes.[46]

46. This collection of six stanzas has absolutely no standard meter or rhyme scheme. Most of the stanzas have six lines, but the fourth is a quatrain, and the final one contains seven lines. Verse 1's meter is 7^3, 6^3, 4^1, 4^1, 4^1, 3^1. Verse 2's meter is 4^2, 4^1, 3^1, 4^1, 4^1, 4^1. And verse 3's meter is 4^2, 4^2, 3^1, 4^1, 4^1, 4^1. The verse that is most irregular is the fourth, which is 3^2, 7^1, 3^1, 7^1. The two verses that are most strongly regular are the last two, which have meters of 4^2, 4^2, 3^1, 4^2, 4^2, 3^1 and 4^2, 4^2, 4^2, 3^1, 4^2, 4^2, 3^1, respectively. All of these meters are irregular and loose. Verse 4 appears to be a loose inversion of *cró cummaisc etir rannaigecht agus sruth di aill,* and the other verses are loose versions of *ochtfhoclach* (Murphy 1961, 56, 70ff). There is very little end rhyme throughout, although there is quite a bit of alliteration. I have mirrored the meters for each stanza and have replicated where possible the alliteration as well.

A tasty, great, hard-cheese collar   [955]
'Round his neck
A bright bridle and its harness,
Butter fresh.

Reins of striped fat on his bridle
Spread all 'round
Full saddlebag with tripe engorged
Gore-stained tripe.

Egg-eater, my page, my horseboy
Has my back
Who challenges him—no boasting—
Meets sure death.

On me a tunic of porridge
Spread all 'round
A slice of tripe and of suet
That bleeds not."[47]

"Off you go now to those delightful, marvelous foods, Mac   [973]
Conglinne!" said the specter, "such as . . .

"Foods, many and exotic   [975]
Steaks, chops from all animals
Red-gold dishes, brown-crusted,
Simmer, bubble out.

47. These four stanzas are clearly meant to follow the meter 8^2, 3^1, 8^2, 3^1, although the poet was occasionally hyper- or hypometric. There is not much internal rhyme or alliteration, and b and d rhyme. This type of meter is called *sétnad ngairit* (Murphy 1961, 50). I have matched the meter of these verses.

Corned beef brisket limitless
Creamy suets, succulent,
And lovely boar loins."[48]

"So be off now to the suets and the soft cheeses!" said the specter.

"Here I go," said Mac Conglinne, "and put the gospels around me."

"Sure," said the specter, "gospels of four-square dry cheese, and I will put my own paternoster on you; no one who wears it is bothered by hunger or greediness."

[988]   And the specter chanted:

"Smooth juicy bacon protect you, Mac Conglinne!
Clotted, yellow-oozing cream protect you, Mac Conglinne,"
    said the specter;
"a cauldron full of gruel protect you, Mac Conglinne," said the
    specter;
"a cooking pot full of porridge protect you, Mac Conglinne,"
    said the specter.

"I swear to God, my creator," said Mac Conglinne, "I would certainly like to go to that fort and drink my fill of the old, sweet, clarified liquors and eat my fill of those vast, wonderful foods."

"If you would really like that," said the specter, "you will have it, and go as I tell you; but if you go, *don't* go astray."

"How can I do that?" asked Mac Conglinne.

48. This verse follows the 7^3, 7^3, 7^3, 5^1, 7^3, 7^3, 5^1 *eochraid* meter that we saw above (see note 30) in the poem that begins "Vision to me revealèd." D and g should rhyme, and there is a great deal of alliteration. I have replicated the meter and some of the alliteration.

46

"That's not hard to say," replied the specter. "Put yourself under the protection and defense of the bold unequaled warriors, the chiefs of the Tribe of Food, so the gravy won't destroy you."

"How, then?" said Mac Conglinne. "Which of the chiefs of the Tribe of Food are the most heroic defenders against the mighty waves of gravy?"

"That's not hard to say," answered the specter. "Lards and cheeses."

"Here I go, then!" said Mac Conglinne. Joyfully, jauntily, [1006] head held high, with nimble feet. The wind that blows across that country, I will not put my back to it, but walk into it headfirst. That's the only way to do it given the heaviness of the sickness, the scarcity of the cure, and the great desire of the healers. I'm off like a shot: swiftly, wildly, impatiently, eagerly, freakily, smoothly, gliding like a fox sneaking past a shepherd, or a peasant who accosts a sleeping queen in her own bed, or a crow toward offal, or a deer cropping a field of winter rye in midsummer. So I hitch up my shirt over my bum, and I move with such swiftness and agility that neither deer fly, gnat nor midge could approach my back door until I have crossed through field, woods, and wilderness on my way to the lake of that fort.

In the port of the lake in front of me, I saw a small boat of [1019] gravy-soaked corned beef varnished with lard, with benches of curds, a prow of suet, the stern of butter, the oarlocks of marrow, and its oars sides of old boar meat. Indeed, the vessel in which we went was steady. Then after that we rowed across the wide plain of Lake New Milk, across stormy seas of whey, through estuaries of mead, through swelling terrifying storm waves of buttermilk, under long-lasting showers of drippings, past woods dewy with meat juice, past a little spring of fatty grease, among islands of soft cheese, past hard rocks of greasy tallow, past headlands of sour curds, past beaches of dry pressed cheese, until we came to the firm, well-balanced landing place between Mount Butter, Lake

Milk, and Curd's Peak, at the mouth of the pass to the land of the Early-Eating people, before the fort of Fáithliaig, the Witch Doctor. Every oar we pulled in Lake New Milk would bring to the surface sea sand made of curds.

[1034]   Then Mac Conglinne shouted at the top of his lungs, "Ho! Ha! Ho! There are no walls here I could not seize!" Hearing that, Fáithliaig, the Witch Doctor, spoke to his people:

"There is a company coming to you tonight, people, namely, Anér Mac Conglinne of the men of Munster, a noble satirist lad training in splendid poetry and music. He must be well served because he is melancholy, shameless, swift, furious, impatient; he is eager for early breakfasts, he is greedy, ravenous, bold, yet he is gentle and true, very easygoing, a good jester; and he is a man quick to express both thanks and displeasure.[49] No surprise there, because he is able both to satirize and to praise in the banqueting hall of a sturdy and clean, courteous, fine, merry house."

[1046]   "Astonishing, indeed, was the retreat I found myself at, with fourteen thousand stakes of smooth, cured bacon surrounding it. There were dense blackthorns at the top of every long stake, made of boiled juicy lard from choice, well-fed boar, in expectation of a battle against the Butter-Lump and Soft-Cheese tribes who were on Lake New Milk, and warring against Fáithliaig, the Witch Doctor. The door was made of tallow held fast by a bolt of sausage. I climbed out of my boat," said Mac Conglinne, "and went to the door at the outer entrance to the fort. I seized a loaf of bread made from the chaff of coarse meal that was by my right hand just outside the outer porch, and I gave a blow with it to the tallow door with its bolt of sausage. I threw the door before me along the outer porch of the fort, and advanced until I reached the

---

49. This comment is a direct reference to satire. For information on satire in medieval Ireland, see the introduction.

big, bright chief enclosure of the great fort. I stuck my ten pointy bright-pink fingernails into the door of smooth cured bacon with its lock of soft-cheese, and I pushed it down and went inside.

"Then I saw the porter. That servant was handsome, and his [1063] name was Bacon-Worshiper, son of Butter-Lover, son of Lard. He had shoes of smooth, mature bacon on his feet; and leggings of potted meat on his shins above that. He had a tunic of corned beef cinched with a belt of salmon skin and a hooded cloak of fat heifer beef. He wore seven butter circlets on his head, each one studded with rows of fresh leeks. On his neck he wore seven intestine amulets, each sealed with boiled lard. The bacon horse he sat on had legs of custard and hooves of coarse oat bread, ears of curds, and eyes of honey. Its breath plumed sour cream from each of its nostrils, and there was an occasional gush of bragget from its bum. The horse's tail was made of dulse, from which seven handfuls were pulled every twenty-four hours. It had a saddle of peerless corned beef on it, with a halter of heifer hide, a collar of old-wether spleen around its neck, and a little bell of soft cheese suspended from the collar with a narrow gut tongue. The horseman held a many-tailed whip: ten sausages made from fat white cows, and every gravy-soaked drop of liquid that fell from the end of each sausage to the ground would be, with half a loaf, more than sufficient for a priest. He also held a slender staff of boiled briarwood in his hand, and every juicy drop that gushed from the end of it, when he turned it down toward the floor, would be enough to fill seven vats.

"Open the retreat to us," said Mac Conglinne. [1091]

"Come on in, then, wretch," replied the porter.

"When I went in," continued Mac Conglinne, "I saw on my left side the slaves of Fáithliaig, the Witch Doctor, wearing furry cloaks and hairy rags of soft custard, with their shovels of hard bread in their hands, clearing away the dung and manure that was on the stone causeway of custard, from the porch of the big house to the outer gateway of the fort. On my right hand I saw Fáithliaig wearing two gauntlets of marbled rump steak on his forearms and hands, setting the house in order, which was completely covered with chitlins from floor to ceiling. When I went into the kitchen, I saw the son of Fáithliaig, the Witch Doctor, with a fish hook of suet in his hands, attached to a fishing line of small fragments of deer marrow, running through a fishing rod of thirty hands of gut and entrails, angling in a pool of lard. He would pull out a flitch of mature bacon or a haunch of corned beef from the lake of lard mixed with honey, onto a bank of curds that was beside him in the kitchen. And it is in that lake that the son of Fáithliaig, the Witch Doctor, drowned, for whom the famous elegy was made:

"Son of Eoghan, fame is your fate," etc.

"Then I went into the big house. As I put my foot over the threshold into the house, I saw a pure white mattress of butter, on which I sat, and I sank in it to the tops of my ears. The eight strongest men in the king's house were hard-pressed to pull me out by the crown of my head.

[1117] "After that I was taken to the place where Fáithliaig, the Witch Doctor himself, was. 'A prayer, a prayer for me!' I said to him.

"'In the name of soft cheese!' he said to me. 'You don't look well at all,' said the Witch Doctor. 'Alas! It is a look of disease. Your hands are yellow, your tongue is spotted, your eyes are gray. Your condition has grown weak and has caused your eyes and your flesh and your joints and your fingernails to swell. The three witches—scarcity and death and famine—have assailed you with sharp beaks of hunger. An eye that does not bless has looked upon you; a plague of serious illness has visited you. Yours is certainly not the appearance of a well-cared-for, milk-fed calf in the hands of a good cook, nor do you have the look of a well-suckled piglet, but that of a badly brought-up boy, poorly fed, and dejected because of it.'

"'That's to be expected,' said Mac Conglinne, 'such is the extent of my sickness, the lack of a cure, the desire for a remedy.'

"'Tell me what ails you, warrior,' said the Witch Doctor. [1131]

"'Sure, I will,' replied Mac Conglinne. 'I am wasting away, being devastated by something that makes me despondent and sluggish, loving entertainment, hating bad provender, desiring early breakfasts, mulling over my many hankerings, including gnawing meat and swallowing up dairy products. The hunger and famine, thirst and voracity are with me even when I eat, so that I cannot control or enjoy my consumption. I am inhospitable and cheap, I refuse to share but am unkind about my own helping, so that I am wearisome to myself and dear to none. I am tormented by hunger, with its twenty-four divisions such as grief, hunger, and thirst, the arrogance to jump the queue before everyone else to get all kinds of food, and all foods disagreeing with me. My wish would be to have an abundance of all the many marvelous foods of the world for my gullet, so that I could fulfill my desire and sate my greed. Alas, then, great is the distress to someone like me, who cannot have any of these.'

"'I give you my word,' said the Witch Doctor, 'this disease is *bad*. Woe to him who happens to be in it, poor creature. But it will not have to be endured much longer. As you have journeyed to my own retreat, my fort at this time, you will take medicine home with you to remedy your disease, and you will be healthy from now on.'

"'What is that?' asked Mac Conglinne. [1150]

"'Indeed, that's not difficult,' replied Fáithliaig. 'When you go home tonight, go to the well and wash your hands, brush your teeth, and comb every single wayward hair on your head neatly. After that, warm yourself before a blazing fire of straight red oak wood, or of eight chunks of ash wood grown beside foothills

51

where little sparrows leave their droppings in a dry hearth, that goes from high to low so that its hot embers warm you, but the flames do not burn you and the smoke doesn't come near you. Spread out a shaggy hide from a yearling calf on the northeast side of the fire, and rest with your side against a bed of bright-white alder wood. Get a swift, white-armed, intelligent, joyful woman to wait on you; she must be of good reputation and affable, red-lipped, womanly, eloquent, from good people, wearing a necklace, cloak, and brooch, with a black hem between the two corners of her cloak, and not affected by sorrow. Three nurses of her own rank in addition to herself. Three sparks of love and playfulness in her countenance, without an expression of sullenness on her brow. A very suitable, pleasant appearance on her; a five-pleated purple cloak on her fastened with a red-gold brooch; a very beautiful broad face; gorgeous blue eyes in her head. Two eyebrows blue-black as beetles above those eyes balanced out by smooth pink cheeks. A thin red mouth, clean white teeth in her head, as if they were pearls. Soft, smooth, and white forearms; a smooth, snowy body; pleasant, shapely thighs; straight, well-proportioned calves; narrow, white-skinned feet; graceful, long-jointed fingers; lovely pink fingernails: that girl should be sprightly in her stride and her gait; as sweet as harp strings should be her gentle speech and conversation, warm and sweet. A woman with no fault or blemish or defect that a keen-sighted, wary observer might find on her from the crown of her head to the sole of her foot.

[1178]   "'Have that woman give you thrice nine helpings, Mac Conglinne, and every helping as big as the egg of a full-grown hen. You must ram the bites into your mouth with a hard shove, and roll your eyes around in your skull while you eat them. You must not spare the eight varieties of grain, Mac Conglinne, wherever you find them: rye, wild oats, coarse barley, buckwheat, wheat, barley, red wheat, and oats. Eat eight loaves from each grain and eight condiments for every loaf and eight relishes for every

52

condiment; and every bite you throw into your mouth should be as big as a heron's egg.

"'Now, off you go to the little pots of fine sweet curds, Mac Conglinne! [1188]

'To fresh pork, to fatty feasts;
to boiled mutton, cooked wethers;
to the choice, oft-discussed bits for which the armies fight—
    corned beef brisket;
to the delicacies of gentlefolk—mead;
to the cure for chest colds—aged, cured bacon;
to gruel's need—sour curds;
to the wish of fair unmarried women—fresh milk;
to a queen's herbs—carrots;
to disadvantaging a visitor—ale;
to the prop of Lent—chicken;
to a broken head—custard;
the hand-to-hand—plain bread;
to a bumpy hearth—pressed cheese;
to a bubbly belch—new ale;
to a priest's favorite—fatty cabbage soup;
to the halt of the hunger of a family—white porridge;
to the double-looped twins—sheep intestines;
to the legal dues of a wall—flitches of bacon;
to the bird of a cross—salt;
to the entrance of an assembly—sweet-smelling apples;
to pearls of a household—hen's eggs;
to a moment of nakedness—kernels.'[50]

50. This list of foods used for various—and often undetermined—purposes is perhaps meant to illustrate exactly what food was desirable at the time. "The legal dues of a wall" may refer to hierarchical status observed when sitting at a banquet

[1205]   "When he had recounted those many foods to me, he pre-
scribed my drop of drink.

"'On top of those foods I advised, I would have you drink a
small sup, Mac Conglinne, not too big, only enough for eighty,
of each of these: very thick milk, milk that is not so thick, flowing
and stiff milk, milk of medium thickness, yellow bubbling milk
that you have to chew and swallow, a drop of milk that makes the
clotted bleat of a ram as it goes down the throat, so that the first
swallow says to the last, "I swear to God, you scabby cur, that if
you come down, I'll go up, for there is no room for the bitchiness
of both of us in this doghouse." Whatever disease seizes you from
now on, Mac Conglinne, I will cure, except one sickness, the dis-
ease of sages and gentlefolk, the best of all diseases, the disease
worth perpetual health: the trots.'

"That's the entire vision."

[1220]   At the enticement of the recounting and the enumeration of
the many unusual and delightful foods in the king's presence, the
lawless beast that inhabited the innermost bowels of Cathal mac
Finguine came forward, until it was licking around the inside of his
mouth, smacking its chops. The student had a large fire beside him.
He put each steak in turn on the fire and then put them one at a
time by the king's mouth. At one point, when a chop was brought
to the king's mouth, the accursed one leaped out and fixed his two
claws into the chop that was in the scholar's hands. Mac Conglinne
carried it with him across the hearth, and threw it under a cauldron
on the other side of the fire, and the cauldron was overturned on it!

———————

table. "The bird of a cross" is unclear, as is the "moment of nakedness" (Jackson
1990, 70).

54

This is where the saying "demon cauldron" comes from, from the demon of gluttony that was in Cathal mac Finguine's gullet being under the cauldron.[51] This is not what the storytellers say—they say that it threw itself down the throat of a priest's servant boy, who was drowned in the water mill's pond at Dún Caín at the harbor mouth of Pichán mac Moíle Finde, in Fir Fhéne. But that is not what is in the books of Cork, which say that it was put in the cauldron, and was burned up under it. "We give thanks to God and to Saint Brigit,"[52] said Mac Conglinne, putting his right palm over his own mouth and his left palm over Cathal's mouth; and they wrapped linen cloths around Cathal's head and carried him out.

"What should we do now?" asked Pichán. [1241]

"Simple," said Mac Conglinne. "Let the armies and the hosts, the kings and queens and people, the herds of cattle and flocks and other herds, and all the gold and silver treasure in the fort be carried away from the fort." And it is said by learned men that nothing of more value than a fly's leg was left in the great, central, royal apartment of the fort except the cauldron on top of the demon's head. And then the house was shut up on him from the outside, and four huge fires were kindled here and there in the house. When the house was a blazing column of fire and the flames were towering, the demon leaped up to the roof-tree of the royal house and the fire could do nothing to him. He settled down on top of the house next door.

"Well, now, Munster men," said Mac Conglinne, "there's your [1252] friend there; and shut your gobs so that I can speak with the infamous meddlesome monk there."

51. This part is an apocryphal story about the etymology of the term in Irish. See Jackson 1990, 70.

52. Saint Brigit was one of the patron saints of Ireland. Her *floruit* is the last half of the fifth and first quarter of the sixth century, and she is associated with Kildare.

"Well, wretch," said Mac Conglinne, "yield to us."

"I will do that," replied the devil, "since I cannot *not* yield: you are a man with the grace of God, vast knowledge, a desire for understanding, assiduous humility, a hunger for every goodness, the favor of the sevenfold Spirit. I am a demon by nature, impermeable, and I will tell you my history. I was eighteen months in the mouth of Cathal to the destruction of Munster and the other southern province besides, and if I had been there another year and a half, I would have destroyed all Ireland. If it were not for the nobility, wisdom, chastity, integrity, and sheer number of the bishops and confessors of the monks of great Cork of Munster, who sent you to seek me; and were it not for the virtue of the words, the pledges, the honor, and the soul of the revered noble king whom you have come to rescue; and were it not for your own nobility, wisdom, chastity, and honor, your vast knowledge, and your training in poetry, I would go into your own throat, so that they would whip you with dog leads and sticks and horsewhips throughout all Ireland, and the disease that would carry you off would be hunger."

[1273] "The sign of the cross between myself and your face!" said Mac Conglinne, and struck at him three times with the Gospels.[53]

And the demon said, "If it were not for Saint Brigit, the little fair woman from the Curragh of the Liffey, I swear to God, Cathal mac Finguine, I would have buried you and taken your soul to hell long before now." And he flew off into the ether after that to join the people of hell.

"What do we do now, Mac Conglinne?" asked Pichán.

---

53. Mac Conglinne is making the sign of the cross as protection for himself; he also uses the Gospels as protection in warding off evil.

"That's not hard," replied Mac Conglinne. "Boil new milk and fresh butter along with honey as a new brew for the king." So it was done. A cauldron for one hundred filled with fully boiled milk was cooked up as a special drink for the king, and it was the first great draft had by Cathal after the demon left. After that a bed was made for the king, with a downy quilt, and musicians and minstrels played from midday to milking time. The king fell into a coma-like sleep. The other chieftains lay around Pichán in as pleasant and dignified a manner as ever before. They had great esteem and respect for the scholar that night. The learned (that is, the storytellers and historians) say that the king slept for three days and nights without waking. But the books of Cork say that he only slept for twenty-four hours.

The king got up the next morning and rubbed his face with his [1294] hands. Each drop of brownish pink dew on his face was no smaller than a highly polished, fragrant apple.

"Where is Mac Conglinne?" asked Cathal.

"Here I am," replied Mac Conglinne.

"Tell me your vision now."

"Surely," said Mac Conglinne.

"However long the tale is today, it will not be as long for me as it was yesterday," said Cathal. "Today is not the same as yesterday." Cathal left good fortune and blessings on every one who would read and preserve the vision.

"Something good should be done for Mac Conglinne," said the chieftains.

"That will be done," said Cathal. "A cow from every courtyard in the province of Munster for him, and an ounce of silver from every householder, a cloak from every monastery, and a sheep from every house from Carn to Cork as well for him. Additionally, he will be given the treasure that is better than any of these, Manchín's small, hooded cloak."

[1307] Then Roennu Ressamnach the Satirist[54] came into the house with his son Cruit-Fhiach, "Harp-Raven," and his daughter Mael Chiar, "Cropped Black-Hair," and made these stanzas:

[1310] Manchín set out—a clear task—
Mac Conglinne to accuse;
It is Manchín who was duped
Out of his hooded cloaklet.

Not too much for Comgán[55] pure
(though not one of our people)
the renowned cloak that I see
is worth thrice seven *cumal*[56]
though the color of a crow
from Cathal, king of Munster.

Also not too much for me
Though gold was in its border
If under his control brought
And stated in pure reason

---

54. Roennu Ressamnach suddenly appears, and he and his children compose a poem in praise of Mac Conglinne and to Manchín's detriment. He may be a satirist; Jackson believes that *ressamnach* is a hapax legomenon, but may be derived from *ressad*, "act of satirizing" (1990, 71).

55. This Comgán is not the same one who appears on page 4.

56. A *cumal* is a basic unit of currency in early Ireland. It is worth the equivalent of one female slave; however, as Fergus Kelly points out in *Early Irish Farming*, it is often a unit of value that "may be realized in gold, silver or land." The most common reference to *cumal*s, though, is in cows; one *cumal* is generally about three milking cows (1997, 592–93).

For prudence, health—Cathal now
Receives the cloak from Manchín.[57]

Then Mac Conglinne was given a cow from every courtyard, an ounce of silver from every householder, a cloak from every monastery, a gold arm ring and a Welsh pony, and a white sheep from every house from Carn to Cork. He also received two-thirds of the right to intercession (and a third from the men of Ireland as well), and a permanent seat at the side of Cathal.[58] All these things were given him, as we have said.

Let this tale be heard by every ear and told by one intelligent [1332] tongue to another, as the sages and venerable men and historians have declared, as is read and written in the books of Cork, as the angel of God explained to Mac Conglinne, as Mac Conglinne himself described it to Cathal mac Finguine and the men of Munster as well. Nothing sorrowful will be heard by anyone who has heard it; it will be a year's protection for him. There are thirty chief benefits attached to this tale, and it is sufficient to use only a few as examples. The married couple who is told this on their first night will not separate without an heir; they will lack neither food nor clothing. The new house, in which it is the first tale told—no corpse will be

---

57. These stanzas are written in the *deibide scáilte* meter, with a syllabic count of 7^1, 7^2, 7^1, 7^2, which is the same meter as the poem that begins "I have heard of eight tonight" (see note 10). I have matched the meter throughout, with occasional alliteration.

58. The right to intercession refers to the commission given an intercessor if successfully advocating for disputed proceeds of someone who otherwise has no proper legal right to those proceeds. See *Dictionary of the Irish Language*, s.v. "impide."

carried out of it, it will not want food or clothing, fire will not burn it. The king who has it recited before a battle or a conflict will have victory. This story should be told at the laying out of liquor or the feeding of a prince or the acceptance of a patrimony or inheritance. The reward for telling this tale is a white-spotted, red-eared cow, a shirt of new linen, a fleecy, woolly cloak with a brooch, from kings and queens, from married couples, from stewards, from princes, to him who can tell and recite it to them.

References

REFERENCES

Ackermann, Elfriede Marie. 1944. *"Das Schlaraffenland" in German Literature and Folksong: Social Aspects of an Earthly Paradise, with an Inquiry into Its History in European Literature.* Chicago: Univ. of Chicago Press.

Adcock, Fleur, ed. and trans. 1994. *Hugh Primas and the Archpoet.* Cambridge: Cambridge Univ. Press.

Adomnán of Iona. 1995. *Life of St. Columba.* Translated by Richard Sharpe. New York: Penguin.

Bhreathnach, Edel, ed. 2005. *The Kingship and Landscape of Tara.* Dublin: Four Courts Press.

Bieler, Ludwig, ed. 1963. *The Irish Penitentials.* Dublin: Dublin Institute for Advanced Studies.

Binchy, D. A. 1970. *Celtic and Anglo-Saxon Kingship.* Oxford: Oxford Univ. Press.

———. 1978. *Corpus Iuris Hibernici.* 6 vols. Dublin: Dublin Institute for Advanced Studies.

Bitel, Lisa. 1990. *Isle of the Saints: Monastic Settlement and Christian Community in Early Ireland.* Ithaca: Cornell Univ. Press.

Breatnach, Liam, ed. 1987. *Uraicecht na Ríar: The Poetic Grades in Early Irish Law.* Dublin: Dublin Institute for Advanced Studies.

———. 1994. "An Mheán-Ghaeilge." In *Stair na Gaeilge,* edited by Kim McCone et al., 221–333. Maigh Nuad: National Univ. of Ireland.

Byrne, Francis J. 2001. *Irish Kings and High Kings.* 2nd ed. Dublin: Four Courts Press.

Carney, James. 1985. *Medieval Irish Lyrics with the Irish Bardic Poet.* Mountrath Portlaois: Dolmen Press.

Clancy, Thomas Owen. 1992. "Mac Steléne and the Eight in Armagh: Identity and Context." *Éigse: A Journal of Irish Studies* 26: 80–91.

Clarke, Austin. 2005. *The Son of Learning.* In *Selected Plays of Austin Clarke,* edited by Mary Shine Thompson, 1–42. Gerrards Cross, Buckinghamshire: Colin Smythe.

D'Ablancourt, Nicolas Perrot. 2004. "Preface to Lucian." Translated by Lawrence Venuti. Originally published 1654. In *The Translation Studies Reader,* edited by Lawrence Venuti, 33–37. 2nd ed. New York: Routledge.

Darling, Gregory. 2006. "A Feast of Satire: Orality and the *Aislinge Meic Conglinne.*" *Foilsiú* 5, no. 1 (Spring): 129–40.

Diamond, Jared. 2005. *Collapse: How Societies Choose to Fail or Succeed.* New York: Viking.

Dictionary of the Irish Language. 1983. Edited by E. G. Quin. Compact ed. Dublin: Royal Irish Academy. Complete dictionary also available online at http://www.dil.ie.

Dillon, Myles. 1946. *The Cycles of the Kings.* Oxford: Oxford Univ. Press.

———, ed. 1953. *Serglige Con Culainn.* Dublin: Dublin Institute for Advanced Studies.

Dryden, John. 1992. "Preface to the *Fables.*" Originally published 1700. In *Theories of Translation: An Anthology of Essays from Dryden to Derrida,* edited by Rainer Schulte and John Biguenet, 26–29. Chicago: Univ. of Chicago Press.

Etchingham, Colmán. 1999. *Church Organisation in Ireland AD 650–1000.* Maynooth: Laigin Publications.

Fallon, Padraic. 1990. "The Vision of Mac Conglinne." In *Irish Drama, 1900–1980,* edited by Cóilín Owens and Joan Radner, 456–538. Washington, D.C.: Catholic Univ. of America Press.

Ford, Patrick K., trans. 1999. "The Vision of Mac Con Glinne." In *The Celtic Poets: Songs and Tales from Early Ireland and Wales,* 112–50. Belmont: Ford and Bailie.

References

Gantz, Jeffrey, trans. 1981a. "Bricriu's Feast." In *Early Irish Myths and Sagas,* 221–55. New York: Penguin.

———. 1981b. "The Destruction of Da Derga's Hostel." In *Early Irish Myths and Sagas,* 61–106. New York: Penguin.

Gray, Elizabeth, ed. and trans. 1982. *Cath Maige Tuired: The Second Battle of Mag Tuired.* London: Irish Texts Society. Also available online from CELT, the Corpus of Electronic Texts, at http://www.ucc.ie/celt.

Gwara, Scott James. 1988. "Gluttony, Lust, and Penance in the B-Text of *Aislinge Meic Conglinne.*" *Celtica* 20: 53–72.

Herbert, Máire. 1996. *Iona, Kells, and Derry: The History and Hagiography of the Monastic* Familia *of Columba.* Dublin: Four Courts Press.

Hughes, Kathleen. 1966. *The Church in Early Irish Society.* Ithaca: Cornell Univ. Press.

Jackson, Kenneth Hurlstone, ed. 1942. "The Adventure of Laeghaire Mac Crimhthainn." *Speculum* 17: 377–89.

———. 1983. "The Historical Grammar of Irish: Some Actualities and Some Desiderata." In *Proceedings of the Sixth International Congress of Celtic Studies,* ed. Gearóid Mac Eoin, 1–18. Dublin: Dublin Institute for Advanced Studies.

———, ed. 1990. *Aislinge Meic Conglinne.* Dublin: Dublin Institute for Advanced Studies.

Jaski, Bart. 2000. *Early Irish Kingship and Succession.* Dublin: Four Courts Press.

Jerome. 2004. "Letter to Pammachius." Translated by Kathleen Davis. Originally written 395. In *The Translation Studies Reader,* edited by Lawrence Venuti, 21–30. 2nd ed. New York: Routledge.

Kelly, Fergus, ed. 1976. *Audacht Morainn.* Dublin: Dublin Institute for Advanced Studies.

———. 1988. *A Guide to Early Irish Law.* Dublin: Dublin Institute for Advanced Studies.

———. 1997. *Early Irish Farming.* Dublin: Dublin Institute for Advanced Studies.

Kelly, Kathleen, trans. 2009. "The Land of Cockaygne." Feb. 26. http://nuweb.neu.edu/kkelly/med/cok.html.

Kinsella, Thomas, trans. 1969. *The Táin*. Oxford: Oxford Univ. Press.

Knott, Eleanor. 1957. *Irish Syllabic Poetry, 1200–1600*. 2nd ed. Dublin: Dublin Institute for Advanced Studies.

Leerssen, Joep. 1994. *The Contention of the Bards (Iomarbhágh na bhFileadh) and Its Place in Irish Political and Literary History*. Subsidiary Series No. 2. Dublin: Irish Texts Society.

Lévi-Strauss, Claude. 1969. *The Raw and the Cooked*. Translated by John Weightman and Doreen Weightman. New York: Harper and Row.

Lucas, Angela. 1995. *Anglo-Irish Poems of the Middle Ages*. Dublin: Columba Press.

Mac Airt, Seán, ed. and trans. 1988. *The Annals of Inisfallen*. Dublin: Dublin Institute for Advanced Studies.

Mac Eoin, Gearóid. 1961. "Das Verbalsystem von *Togail Troi* (H. 2. 17)." *Zeitschrift für Celtische Philologie* 28: 73–136, 149–223.

Mac Mathúna, Séamus. 1985. *Immram Brain: Bran's Journey to the Land of the Women*. Tübingen: Niemeyer.

Mac Shamhráin, Ailbhe Séamus. 1996. *Church and Polity in Pre-Norman Ireland: The Case of Glendalough*. Maynooth: An Sagart.

McCone, Kim. 1990. *Pagan Past and Christian Present in Early Irish Literature*. Maynooth Monographs 3. Maynooth: National Univ. of Ireland.

———. 1997. *The Early Irish Verb*. 2nd ed. Maynooth: An Sagart.

———. 2005. *A First Old Irish Grammar and Reader Including an Introduction to Middle Irish*. Maynooth: National Univ. of Ireland.

McLaughlin, Róisín. 2008. *Early Irish Satire*. Dublin: Dublin Institute for Advanced Studies.

McManus, Damian. n.d. "History of the Language II: Middle Irish." Unpublished.

Melia, Daniel F. 2006. "Food, Gluttony, and Power in 12th Century Ireland." 26th Harvard Celtic Colloquium, Harvard Univ., Cambridge, Mass., Oct. 6.

References

———. 2007. "Food, Power, and Exchange in 12th Century Ireland." 30th Annual CSANA (Celtic Studies Association of North America) Conference, Univ. of Cincinnati, Apr. 13.

Mercier, Vivian. 1962. *The Irish Comic Tradition*. Oxford: Clarendon Press.

Meroney, Howard. 1950. "Studies in Early Irish Satire I." *Journal of Celtic Studies* 1: 199–226.

———. 1953. "Studies in Early Irish Satire II." *Journal of Celtic Studies* 2: 59–130.

Meyer, Kuno, ed. and trans. 1889. "Echtra Nerai." *Revue Celtique* 10: 212–28.

———, ed. and trans. 1894. *Hibernica Minora, Being a Fragment of an Old Irish Treatise on the Psalter*. Oxford: Clarendon Press.

———, ed. and trans. 1974 [1892]. *Aislinge Meic Conglinne: The Vision of MacConglinne, a Middle-Irish Wonder Tale*. Reprint, New York: Lemma Publishing.

Murphy, Gerard. 1961. *Early Irish Metrics*. Dublin: Royal Irish Academy.

Nagy, Joseph Falaky. 1985. *The Wisdom of the Outlaw: The Boyhood Deeds of Finn in Gaelic Narrative Tradition*. Berkeley and Los Angeles: Univ. of California Press.

———. 1997. *Conversing with Angels and Ancients: Literary Myths of Medieval Ireland*. Ithaca: Cornell Univ. Press.

Ó Cathasaigh, Tomás. 1977. *The Heroic Biography of Cormac mac Airt*. Dublin: Dublin Institute for Advanced Studies.

Ó Corráin, Donncha. 1973. "Dál Cais—Church and Dynasty." *Ériu* 24: 52–63.

O Daly, Máirín. 1975. *Cath Maige Mucrama*. London: Irish Texts Society.

Ó hUiginn, Ruairí. 1992. "The Background and Development of *Táin Bó Cúailnge*." In *Aspects of "The Táin,"* edited by J. P. Mallory, 29–67. Belfast: December Publications.

Ó Riain, Pádraig, ed. 1994. *Beatha Bharra: Saint Finbarr of Cork, the Complete Life*. London: Irish Texts Society.

Oskamp, H. P. A. 1974. "Echtra Condla." *Études Celtiques* 14: 207–28.

O'Sullivan, Catherine Marie. 2004. *Hospitality in Medieval Ireland, 900–1500*. Dublin: Four Courts Press.

Owens, Cóilín, and Joan Radner. 1990. *Irish Drama, 1900–1980*. Washington, D.C.: Catholic Univ. Press.

Picard, Jean-Michel, and Yolande de Pontfarcy, trans. 1989. *The Vision of Tnugdal*. Dublin: Four Courts Press.

Pleij, Herman. 1997. *Dreaming of Cockaigne: Medieval Fantasies of the Perfect Life*. Translated by Diane Webb. New York: Columbia Univ. Press, 2001.

Plummer, Charles, ed. and trans. 1968a [1910]. *Vita Sanctorum Hiberniae*. 2 vols. Reprint, Oxford: Oxford Univ. Press.

———, ed. and trans. 1968b [1922]. *Bethada Náem nÉrenn: Lives of Irish Saints*. 2 vols. Reprint, Oxford: Oxford Univ. Press.

Robinson, Fred Norris. 1912. "Satirists and Enchanters in Early Irish Literature." In *Studies in the History of Religions Presented to Crawford Howell Toy*, 95–130. New York: Macmillan.

Sayers, William. 1994. "Diet and Fantasy in Eleventh-Century Ireland: *The Vision of Mac Con Glinne*." *Food and Foodways* 6, no. 1: 1–17.

Schleiermacher, Friedrich. 2004. "On the Different Methods of Translating." Translated by Susan Bernofsky. Originally published 1813. In *The Translation Studies Reader*, edited by Lawrence Venuti, 43–63. 2nd ed. New York: Routledge.

Selmer, Carl. 1989 [1959]. *Navigatio Sancti Brendani Abbatis*. Reprint, Dublin: Four Courts Press.

Sharpe, Richard. 1992. "Churches and Communities in Early Medieval Ireland: Towards a Pastoral Model." In *Pastoral Care Before the Parish*, edited by John Blair and Richard Sharpe, 81–109. Leicester: Leicester Univ. Press.

Shaw, Francis, ed. 1934. *Aislinge Óenguso*. Dublin: Browne and Nolan.

Stokes, Whitley, ed. and trans. 1887. "The Siege of Howth." *Revue Celtique* 8: 47–64.

———, ed. 1888a. "The Voyage of Mael Duin." *Revue Celtique* 9: 447–95.

———, ed. 1888b. "The Voyage of Snedgus and Mac Riagla." *Revue Celtique* 9: 14–25.

———, ed. 1889. "The Voyage of Mael Duin." *Revue Celtique* 10: 50–95.

———, ed. 1893. "The Voyage of the hÚi Corra." *Revue Celtique* 14: 22–69.

———, ed. and trans. 1903. "The Wooing of Luaine and Death of Athirne." *Revue Celtique* 24: 270–87.

———, ed. 2000 [1862]. *Three Irish Glossaries*. Reprint, Lampeter: Llanerch Press.

Venuti, Lawrence. 2004a. "Foundational Statements." In *The Translation Studies Reader*, edited by Lawrence Venuti, 13–20. 2nd ed. New York: Routledge.

———. 2004b. "Translation, Community, Utopia." In *The Translation Studies Reader*, edited by Lawrence Venuti, 482–502. 2nd ed. New York: Routledge.

Whicher, George F., trans. 1949. *The Goliard Poets: Medieval Latin Songs and Satires*. Cambridge: Harvard Univ. Press.

Wiley, Dan M., ed. 2008. *Essays on the Early Irish King Tales: Rígscéla Éirenn*. Dublin: Four Courts Press.

Zeydel, Edwin H., trans. 1966. *Vagabond Verse: Secular Latin Poems of the Middle Ages*. Detroit: Wayne State Univ. Press.

LAHNEY PRESTON-MATTO teaches in the English Department at Adelphi University in Garden City, New York. She has published several articles on the intersections between law, gender, and agency in medieval Ireland.